no bake makery

no bake makery

more than 80 two-bite treats
made with lovin', not an oven

CRISTINA SUAREZ KRUMSICK

PHOTOGRAPHS BY JEREMY KRUMSICK

GRAND CENTRAL
Life & Style

NEW YORK   BOSTON

Unless otherwise noted, all photos are by Jeremy Krumsick.

Photo credits:
Pages 8–10, sprinkles, copyright Ruth Black
Pages 16–17: spatula, copyright Charlene Bayerle; scoop, copyright Gavran 333; mixer, copyright M. Unal Ozmen; cupcake wrappers, copyright Brooke Becker
Page 104, whipped cream, copyright Shira Raz
Page 134, raspberries, copyright barbaradudzinka

Designed by Alissa Faden

Grand Central Life & Style
Hachette Book Group
237 Park Avenue
New York, NY 10017

www.HachetteBookGroup.com

Printed in the United States of America

Q-MA

First Edition: May 2013
10 9 8 7 6 5 4 3 2 1

Grand Central Life & Style is an imprint of Grand Central Publishing.
The Grand Central Life & Style name and logo are trademarks of Hachette Book Group, Inc.

The Hachette Speakers Bureau provides a wide range of authors for speaking events.
To find out more, go to www.HachetteSpeakersBureau.com or call (866) 376-6591.

The publisher is not responsible for websites (or their content) that are not owned by the publisher.

Library of Congress Cataloging-in-Publication Data
Krumsick, Cristina Suarez.
  No bake makery : more than 80 two-bite treats made with lovin', not an oven / Cristina Suarez Krumsick ; photographs by Jeremy Krumsick.
      pages cm
  Includes index.
  Summary: "From the proprietor and chef of Brooklyn's NO BAKE MAKERY comes an original cookbook filled with recipes for delicious, mini desserts that don't require an oven."—Provided by the publisher
  ISBN 978-1-4555-2513-3 (hardcover)
  1. Desserts. I. Krumsick, Jeremy. II. Title.
  TX773.K716 2013
  641.86—dc23
                        2012041779

For Jeremy

Contents

Introduction

ABOUT ME

I was born in Miami, Florida, into a very loud, very wonderful Cuban family. As anyone who's ever met a Cuban knows: We love food.

But what I've discovered—and it took me awhile to put my finger on it—is that what Cubans actually like most is *feeding* people. The best part of cooking is satisfying hunger in those you love, whether it's with a hearty meal or a sweet bite. What every passionate cook in my family really enjoys most is feeding the people he or she loves. *Pleasing* people. *Hosting* people. And that's exactly how I feel too.

I didn't realize the bug had rubbed off on me in such a serious way until I graduated from college and moved in with my then boyfriend (now husband). Suddenly I was coming home from my first "real" job and putting on an apron every single night. I am no trained chef, but I have spent countless hours in the kitchen. And I'm talking tiny, New York City, my-counter-doubles-as-my-desk kind of kitchens. My first NYC apartment was a "one bedroom," 400-square-foot hole-in-the-wall. The bathroom was in the bedroom, the AC unit was in the bathroom, the closets were in the living room, and the kitchen was maybe five feet by three feet. People aren't kidding when they talk about how small Manhattan apartments are! While this situation wasn't ideal for many reasons, it did teach me that anyone can make my recipes, *anywhere*.

The minute the first gust of fall hit, the hosting gene kicked in. It was barely past Labor Day when I started planning a Christmas party and, of course, a Christmas party menu. I went to some pretty extreme measures to ensure that the party was fabulous, including trekking tons of apple cider, port, and cognac through a near blizzard. My grand plan included popping chocolate chip cookies into the (barely functional) oven toward the end of the night and filling the room with an irresistible smell before finally sending people off with a late-night munchy. The oven must have been *extra*-tired that night—the cookies took more than two hours to bake (instead of just twenty minutes), so only the very last of our guests were served half-baked treats. Despite the mishap, the party was a big success in a tiny space.

Eventually we moved to Brooklyn, and two things changed my life: a kitchen island (four feet by two feet of dedicated counter space with storage

underneath!) and a patio (we can have more than four people over at a time!). Suffice it to say, the hosting itch became even itchier. Seventy-four and sunny meant nothing to me but a barbecue. And a barbecue meant nothing but a menu. And a menu meant fun in the kitchen. And what's more fun than serving bite-size sweets once the coals stop burning?

I am not interested in achieving culinary greatness with overly complicated or fancy food; in fact, all it takes to make me happy is the simple act of people coming back for seconds. Admittedly, I probably care a little too much about what people think of my food. I notoriously stare at my husband when he takes his first bite, waiting to read his face to see whether he digs it or not. It drives him nuts!

I think when you love something so much that you become obsessed with it or can't stop thinking about it, that's when you know you need to take it a step further. For me, that step was No Bake Makery.

ABOUT NO BAKE MAKERY

I launched No Bake Makery in August 2011 as part of my ongoing quest to be Martha Stewart—on a budget and with a day job—and as a labor of love to satisfy my passion for sweets and cute things. This aspiration, in combination with a bit of know-how from my "real life" in book publicity—often cookbook publicity—gave me the grounding I needed to jump-start a sweets business.

The idea started whirling around in my mind early that summer. I had a bunch of get-togethers in my Brooklyn apartment, and serving tiny, easy desserts was a recurring theme—I consider offering sweets a hosting imperative, but I *hate* overheating a summer kitchen. One summer night around 4:30 a.m. I woke up to nonstop "bite" ideas. Banana, peanut butter, wafer bites...cherry, coconut, almond bites...peanut butter cookie bites! (I guess worse thoughts could keep you up at night, right?) I am normally a really deep sleeper, so I knew this meant business. Literally.

I finally got back to bed around 6 a.m., and when my alarm went off at 9 a.m., I was hungry and ready to get started on my new venture. It seemed simple: a series of no bake desserts. All bite-size. All yummy. All adorable. All reasonably priced.

By December 2011—just four months after my company's launch—I had made more than three thousand bites to fulfill the orders that had poured in from all over the United States. I was also catering events from weddings and charity fund-raisers to toddlers' birthday parties and baby showers to fancy fashion parties. These events went so well that I eventually decided to focus solely on them, specializing in fine-tuning treats for every occasion, in both flavor and presentation.

I began to build a following and started to receive tons of questions: "How did you come up with the idea?"; "Do you even have an oven in your apartment?"; and most frequently, of course, "How can I make these myself?"

This book is the happy response to those inquiries.

Cristina

no bake makery

Welcome

TO

No Bake Land

What You'll Need

Working with Chocolate

Melting and Tempering

The Wilton Helper

Dipping

Drizzling

Within these pages you'll discover no bake recipes that are fun to make, even better to eat, and adorable to look at. While all the recipes are uncomplicated, they range in simplicity: from three ingredients with just three steps to twelve ingredients with more than ten steps. You'll find truffles, bark, clusters, pies, cakes, ice creams, puddings, ice pops, cookies, candies, and even some breakfast-items-turned-desserts. They can be used for any occasion, from lunch-box snacks to after-dinner treats. Most of them are so charming, they can even be considered an edible accessory to whatever shindig you're throwing. In fact, I've included a tool to make using this book even easier. You can consult the chart on page 14 for inspiration in choosing appropriate recipes for different guests and holidays. In addition, you'll see a gluten-free or gluten-free option (on page 18) throughout the book. No matter whom you're baking for or why, these recipes all have one thing in common: They simply do not make use of the big, hot, boxy appliance that sits smack in the middle of your kitchen.

But before we get any further, let me make it clear that I have nothing at all against ovens. Actually, I think they're essential. Without them we couldn't enjoy delicious breads, roasts, pizzas, and let's not forget, Thanksgiving turkey. I use my oven *all* the time! Promise. I have decided, however, that what you do not need one for is dessert.

You know how some people love to bake and others prefer to cook? Well, I think I know how the divide came about. When cooking savory food, you have some creative freedom in the kitchen. Don't have cilantro handy? Skip it! Your guac will be just fine. But if you don't have enough flour when you're baking, forget it. No cake for you. None at all. Most baked desserts require that you follow a recipe *so* exact that making even one measurement mistake could result in your scone becoming a cookie. Just when you were really craving that scone! These two methods for working in the kitchen appeal to two different kinds of people.

This book is for the cook who loves sweets but hates to bake. It's about exciting flavor combinations and reinventing treats that people have loved for ages. The greatest thing about no baking is that as with cooking, you can play around with the ingredients. We follow rules all day! Fill out this form. Go to that meeting. Write this paper. It goes on and on. When we get home and into the kitchen, we should be able to play.

We can easily make food even more playful by making it tiny. A two-bite treat is simply more appealing than a bigger one. Not only are they better-looking, but they are also more accessible and less ridden with guilt. Why two? Well, one is definitely never enough, and eating too much dessert is never a good idea. The obvious answer is two bites! Plus, they are cute. And cute is key.

So now we know *what* we are in store for: two-bite treats, made with lovin', not an oven. But *how*? I'll show you! You'll find helpful tips in this chapter and throughout the book that will have you no bake making in no time.

NEED SOME
INSPIRATION?

WHAT YOU'LL NEED

Here is a list of items that will come in handy throughout the book. I've broken them down into items you might have, those you'll most likely have, and some that are not completely necessary but may make things easier.

You may already have...

> **KITCHEN THERMOMETER:** Eventually you won't need this tool when you become a tempering pro, but it will be a huge help when you're starting out. I use the Taylor 9842 Commercial Waterproof Digital Thermometer. It's super-cheap and has a wide range (–40 to 450°F). This means you can use it for all sorts of recipes, from tempering chocolate to making sugar candy to frying donuts.

> **MICROWAVE-SAFE BOWLS:** All different sizes will come in handy. You can buy great sets at Bed Bath & Beyond, Target, or any home goods store. You'll use these for melting, mixing, whipping—you name it.

> **MELON BALLER OR 1-INCH COOKIE SCOOP:** Make sure it holds 2 teaspoons of cookie dough. This will help you keep your treats to two bites and help you keep them all the same size. It will be most useful for truffles and mini pies.

> **FOOD PROCESSOR:** Best. Kitchen. Tool. Ever. A standard 7-cup processor is ideal, but if you have a mini processor or a Magic Bullet, that works too—you may just have to work in batches. The Vitamix and other blenders can also work, but their narrowness is a little inconvenient for cookie and cracker processing. This one is worth investing in—you'll use it for everything!

> **COOKIE SHEET**

> **MEDIUM NONSTICK SAUTÉ PAN**

> **RUBBER SPATULA:** I have small, medium, and large versions, and I use them all the time!

> **WHISK**

> **MINI MUFFIN TIN:** Slots should be 1¾ inches in diameter.

> **MINI MUFFIN TIN LINERS:** Foil or paper is fine.

> **SILICONE ICE CUBE TRAYS:** I specifically recommend silicone ice cube trays or candy molds to make your life (your ice pop–making life, that is) *much* easier. These will allow your treats to pop out smoothly, and they come in really cute shapes and sizes—everything from flowers to little sombreros! You can find them at Bed Bath & Beyond, Target, and baking supply stores.

> **SIFTER:** This helps make your powdered sugar appliqué look really clean and professional.

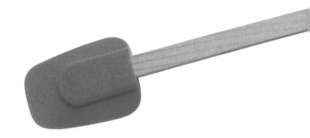

You probably already have...

> **CUTTING BOARD**

> **PLASTIC SANDWICH BAGS** to drizzle toppings

> **8 BY 8-INCH BAKING PAN AND 9 BY 13-INCH BAKING PAN:** Don't worry. These won't ever go into the oven!

> **MICROWAVE-SAFE MEASURING CUPS:** I recommend having both a 1-cup and a 2-cup measure.

> **SHARP KNIFE:** You'll need one to cut dry chocolate. It'll also help to make perfect cuts for bars, bark, and clusters.

> **DINNER FORKS:** These will help you dip truffles into chocolate.

> **WAX PAPER**

> **ALUMINUM FOIL**

> **PLASTIC WRAP**

You don't need but could use...

> **DOUBLE BOILER:** This has two connecting pots situated one on top of the other. The top pot is for the chocolate and the bottom pot is for water. An alternative to using a double boiler is to place a clear, heatproof bowl (for the chocolate) over a pot of boiling water. However, this strategy may be a little tricky if you don't have a clear bowl, because you have to make sure the bottom of the bowl doesn't actually touch the boiling water. If the bowl touches the water, the chocolate will burn.

> **TONGS**

> **ELECTRIC MIXER** (standing and/or handheld)

> **FOOD SCALE**

You definitely have...

> Your own hands—you can even use a friend's!

WORKING WITH CHOCOLATE

Who doesn't love chocolate? It's (almost) everyone's favorite, but it can be a bit tricky to work with sometimes. There are a couple of chocolate techniques and tricks that you'll see pop up quite often throughout this book. They are really quite easy to learn and master, but you'll find icons that will refer you back here in case you need a little reminder.

TEMPER	
WILTON	
DIPPING	
DRIZZLE	

Quality of Chocolate

If you are going to splurge on anything, splurge on chocolate. Chocolate chips are often cheaper than block or chunk chocolate, but they are a pain in the butt to work with. They are meant for baking, which we've already decided we aren't doing here. Most chips have additives that help them keep their shape during baking, which affects the tempering process. As you'll soon see, we'll be doing a bit of that. The ingredient list of a high-quality block or chunk chocolate contains primarily cocoa solids and cocoa butter in varying proportions. Not only is it easier to work with, but it also makes your treats prettier and even more delicious.

When you see this icon, the recipe is gluten-free. **GF**

When you see this icon, I'll tell you how to make the recipe gluten-free. **GF**

🍫 MELTING AND TEMPERING

While chocolate can be like a comforting friend, it's also quite sensitive and requires handling with finesse. In order for it to harden and shape properly, it must go through a process called tempering. Tempering means exactly what it sounds like: melting and cooling chocolate until the temperature is just right. In doing so, you'll ensure that the cocoa butter in the chocolate hardens into a uniform crystal structure. Chocolate that is not tempered might turn out cloudy, too thick, or very sticky. Tempered chocolate, on the other hand, is shiny, smooth, and perfectly snappable. For this reason, tempering is necessary only in recipes where chocolate is used for the *outside* layer of a treat. If this is the case, you'll see a temper icon on the page and you should follow the complete process below. If you don't see the icon and simply need to melt chocolate, just follow steps 1 and 2.

One important tidbit to remember is that 1 cup melted chocolate equals about 1½ cups dry chocolate roughly chopped into quarter-size pieces. The dry chocolate should weigh about 9.25 ounces on a food scale.

Steps for melting and tempering:

1. Break or roughly cut your chocolate into quarter-size pieces to prepare it for melting.

2. Place the chocolate in a double boiler or a clear, heatproof bowl over a pot of simmering water. Keep the water simmering and stir the chocolate with a spatula until it is melted. If using a microwave, set it on high power and melt your chocolate in a microwave-safe bowl in 30-second intervals, stirring after each interval.

3. Once it's melted, check the temperature using a cooking thermometer. Your chocolate should be between 110 and 115°F.

4. Transfer the melted chocolate into a clean, room-temperature bowl.

5. Stir, stir, and stir some more. Be sure to mix the melted chocolate in with some of the crystallized chocolate on the edges that is cooling faster.

6. When your thermometer reads 88 to 90°F, your chocolate is ready to go to work!

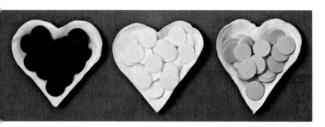

 THE WILTON HELPER

If the instructions on tempering chocolate make you roll your eyes, sigh, or feel confused at all, look out for this icon in the book. Wilton Candy Melts are special little coating helpers that are incredibly easy to melt and easy to dip your treats into. As opposed to regular chocolate, these require no tempering at all. Before use, they simply need to be melted in a microwave-safe bowl in 30-second intervals, and stirred after each interval. They also dry at room temperature, so they quicken your no bake making time too.

If you choose the Wilton Helper over melting and tempering, be sure to measure out the same quantity of candy melts as the amount of chocolate the recipe calls for. For example, if the recipe calls for 1½ cups of dark chocolate chopped from a block into quarter-size pieces, you can just measure out 1½ cups of quarter-size Wilton Candy Melts.

You can find these helpful little guys at your local home goods or craft store, but generic brands look the same and work just as well; these are available at your local baking supply store.

If you want to make your treats a fun color like purple or yellow, you'll definitely want to use these. Adding liquid food coloring to your chocolate ruins its consistency, so I highly recommend avoiding it. In fact, if even one drop gets in it, you'll probably have to discard it. Alternatively, you can find *powdered* food coloring at a baking supply store to stain your chocolate with.

DIPPING

When you are getting ready to dip treats into chocolate, make sure your chocolate is either tempered or specifically meant for candy coating (like the Wilton Candy Melts). Mix your melted chocolate with a fork right before you begin dipping to make sure it's thin enough. If it doesn't drip off your fork easily, it's probably too thick. Add ¼ teaspoon vegetable oil at a time and mix well until your chocolate is thin and slick enough to work with.

Also, be sure to work with a bowl or cup that's neither too narrow nor too wide. Measuring cups tend to be perfect for dipping these two-bite treats.

Here is the tried-and-true technique I like to use:

Slide a dinner fork under your treat and lower it into the melted chocolate. Submerge your treat so it's just under the surface of the chocolate; then lift it out immediately. Tap the fork gently several times against the side of the bowl and slide the bottom of the fork over the lip of the bowl to remove excess chocolate. Transfer the treat to your prepared baking sheet, tilting your fork slightly so the treat glides right off.

⊙ DRIZZLING

Of course baking supply stores offer tons of fancy tools for drizzling chocolate, but there is no piping bag or squeeze bottle that can compete with…a plastic sandwich bag! Yep, that's right.

All you have to do is scoop a couple of tablespoons of chocolate into the corner of a good ol' sandwich bag. Next, heat a cup or bowl of room-temperature water in the microwave for about a minute. Dip the chocolate-filled corner of the bag into the water until the chocolate is completely melted, mashing it around with your fingers to evenly distribute it. You may need to reheat the water and repeat.

Once the chocolate is completely melted, dry off your bag. Using your hands, make sure the chocolate-filled corner has no air bubbles in it and then snip off a tiny piece of the tip with your kitchen scissors. Twist down the top of your bag so the chocolate doesn't move upward. Apply pressure to the chocolate corner and you're drizzling!

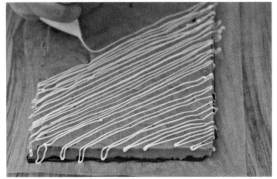

Now it's time to put all these techniques—and more—into action. Here we go!

Truffles

Lil' Peanut

Cinnalmond Bite

Colorful Crunch

Apple Granola Bite

Coo Coo for Coconut

Fruity Two-Bite

Bite o' Joe

Cinni Minni

The Clary

Maple Pecan Bite

Chocolate Chip Cookie
Remix

Booze Balls

The Cookie Union

Minty

Ah, yummy sweet bites of goodness. I have always liked truffles, but I began *loving* them upon discovering the cookie truffle. My friend Ariele and I were sitting on the L train heading home to Brooklyn early in the summer. It was just that time of year when New York City becomes unbearably hot and any thoughts of turning on your oven melt away. We were brainstorming what to make for a last-minute barbecue I was having the next night at my apartment and narrowed it down to the most basic cookie ball possible: crushed Oreos mixed with cream cheese. Ariele has a taste for very classic food and voted with enthusiasm that I make these for dessert. Why not put an interesting twist on a treat everyone already loves? I went home and did just that, adding peanut butter to some, coconut to others, and getting really creative with my sprinkle appliqué.

Suffice it to say, the treats were delicious and *so* cute. All of my friends loved them. My Korean friend, Jin, whose lost-in-translation vocabulary often results in quotable commentary, repeatedly called them "so beautiful," as if she was referring to a gorgeous, colorful sunset. Little did I know, that night was the beginning of a long and enduring cookie truffle relationship—a relationship so tight that my initial focus with No Bake Makery was sharing these with the world. Eventually these cookie truffles turned into cookie trouble—it's bad news to have hundreds of these in your refrigerator at a time!

Over the course of a few more barbecues I came up with different recipes by adjusting my truffle elements:

- Dry agents (like cookies and crackers)
- Sticking agents (like honey, milk, cream cheese, and jam)
- Beautifiers (the pretty stuff on top that hints at what's inside)

I've narrowed the selection in this chapter down to my favorites, which I want to share with you.

Enjoy!

lil' peanut

EVERY TIME I GO TO one of NYC's many self-serve frozen yogurt spots (I'm obsessed with 16 Handles!), I end up overloading on all things peanut. I usually go for peanut butter yogurt with a bit of vanilla for good measure. When I hit the toppings bar, nothing appeals to me more than the peanut M&M'S, Reese's Pieces, and a little swirl of chocolate syrup on top. I took this clear winner of a combination and translated it into this perfectly peanutty two-bite truffle.

⬦⬦⬦⬦⬦⬦⬦⬦⬦⬦**MAKES ABOUT 25 TREATS**⬦⬦⬦⬦⬦⬦⬦⬦⬦⬦

Line a cookie sheet with wax paper and set aside.

In a food processor, process the cookies with the chocolate chips until fine crumbs form, about 1 minute. Add the honey and cream cheese and process until a dough begins to form, about 30 seconds.

Transfer the dough to a clean bowl.

Take about a quarter-size ball of dough and flatten it out to wrap around 1 peanut M&M, forming a 1-inch ball; repeat with the remaining dough and M&M'S, placing the balls on the prepared cookie sheet. The candy centers help to make these bites perfectly round. Refrigerate uncovered for 30 minutes.

Melt and temper the chocolate (or melt Wilton Candy Melts). Dip the balls into the melted milk chocolate and place them back on the cookie sheet. Top each with a single Reese's Piece. Refrigerate for 30 minutes, or until solid.

10 peanut butter sandwich cookies (I like Nutter Butters)

¾ cup milk chocolate chips

1½ tablespoons honey

2 tablespoons cream cheese, softened (I recommend using light or ⅓ fat)

1 small package peanut M&M'S

1½ cups milk chocolate chopped into quarter-size pieces (or Wilton Candy Melts)

1 small package Reese's Pieces

cinnalmond bite

12 chocolate sandwich cookies
(Joe-Joes are my favorite)

1 cup Cinnamon Toast Crunch
cereal (store brand or General
Mills)

5 tablespoons unsalted sliced
almonds

2 teaspoons ground cinnamon

2 tablespoons honey

¼ cup almond milk

1 teaspoon sea salt

1½ cups dark chocolate chopped
into quarter-size pieces (or Wilton
Candy Melts)

MY PARENTS NEVER KEPT *too much cereal in the house when I was growing up, so when sleepover age hit, I was beyond excited to have access to boxes upon boxes of it. The cereal that stuck with me the most was Cinnamon Toast Crunch. When I first tried it, I remember thinking:* This is dessert. *Now I mix almonds, Cinnamon Toast Crunch, and honey with a little milk for dessert. I didn't think this combination could get much better...until I morphed it into the Cinnalmond Bite.*

◇◇◇◇◇◇◇◇◇◇◇◇◇◇◇**MAKES ABOUT 25 TREATS**◇◇◇◇◇◇◇◇◇◇◇◇◇◇◇

Line a cookie sheet with wax paper and set aside.

In a food processor, process the cookies and cereal until fine crumbs form, about 1 minute. Add 3 tablespoons of the almond slices and 1 teaspoon of the cinnamon and process for another 30 seconds. Add the honey and almond milk and process until a dough begins to form, about 30 seconds. Transfer the mixture to a clean bowl.

Roll the dough into 1-inch balls (see box, page 34). Place on the prepared cookie sheet and refrigerate uncovered for 45 minutes.

Roughly chop the remaining 2 tablespoons almond slices and place them in a small bowl. Mix in the remaining 1 teaspoon cinnamon and the salt to make your cinnalmond mixture. Set aside.

Melt and temper the chocolate (or melt Wilton Candy Melts). Dip each ball into the dark chocolate and place back on the cookie sheet. Sprinkle with the cinnalmond mixture. Refrigerate until solid, about 1 hour.

colorful crunch

THESE HAVE CELEBRATION WRITTEN ALL *over them. Next time you are hosting a birthday party, serve them on a cake stand. I promise that nobody will miss the cake—these truffles are gooey and cakey on the outside, and the inside has a little crunchy and fruity surprise. You may want to double the recipe…kids are drawn to them and adults love the throwback flavors!*

◇◇◇◇◇◇◇◇◇◇◇◇◇◇◇**MAKES ABOUT 20 TREATS**◇◇◇◇◇◇◇◇◇◇◇◇◇◇◇

Line a cookie sheet with wax paper and set aside.

To make the inside:
Heat the butter in a medium saucepan over low heat until melted, about 1 minute. Add the marshmallows and stir with a spatula until completely melted, about 5 minutes. Remove from the heat. Add the fruity cereal and mix until evenly distributed. Transfer to a plate and let cool for 5 minutes—no longer. The mixture will be difficult to roll if you let it sit too long. The mixture should still be warm but not too hot to handle.

Using your hands, roll the mixture into ½-inch balls and place on the prepared cookie sheet.

To make the outside:
Process the cookies in a food processor until fine crumbs form, about 1 minute. Add the honey and cream cheese and process until a dough begins to form, about 30 seconds.

Wrap each fruity cereal ball with dough to form 1-inch balls, then place them back on the prepared cookie sheet. The inside cereal balls help make the bites perfectly round. Refrigerate uncovered for 30 minutes.

While the balls are in the refrigerator, melt and temper the white chocolate (or melt Wilton Candy Melts). Dip the balls into the melted white chocolate and return them to the prepared cookie sheet. Using your fingers, sprinkle each truffle with nonpareils. Refrigerate until solid, about 1 hour.

INSIDE
1 teaspoon unsalted butter

1 cup mini marshmallows

1 cup fruity cereal (I like Fruity Pebbles)

OUTSIDE
14 chocolate sandwich cookies (Joe-Joes are my favorite)

1½ tablespoons honey

2 tablespoons cream cheese, softened (I recommend light or ⅓ fat)

1½ cups white chocolate chopped into quarter-size pieces (or Wilton Candy Melts)

¼ cup nonpareils

Stick to lowfat or light cream cheese when making these or any truffles that are coated in chocolate. If you use full-fat cream cheese, the extra oil may crack your coating.

apple granola bite

15 vanilla sandwich cookies (Joe-Joes are my favorite)

2 tablespoons unsweetened applesauce

1 teaspoon ground cinnamon

1 cup pumpkin spice granola (or plain granola with ½ teaspoon pumpkin spice mixed in)

1½ cups white chocolate chopped into quarter-size pieces (or Wilton Candy Melts)

GROWING UP IN MIAMI, *I was deprived of the changing seasons. So when I went to Boston for college and experienced my first fall foliage, I was truly taken aback. Not only were the leaves all the colors of a fiery sunset, but the season also came along with new activities that I'd never taken part in before: apple picking and visiting pumpkin patches. After that first fall in New England, I was hooked on seasonal festivities—particularly those involving people gathering to celebrate the fruits and vegetables in season. If that kind of party doesn't call for a no bake dedication, I don't know what does! With sweet hints of apple and pumpkin spice, this little bite has the season written all over it. Fall, this one is for you.*

◇◇◇◇◇◇◇◇◇◇◇◇◇◇◇◇◇**MAKES ABOUT 20 TREATS**◇◇◇◇◇◇◇◇◇◇◇◇◇◇◇◇◇

Line a cookie sheet with wax paper and set aside.

Process the cookies in a food processor until fine crumbs form, about 1 minute. Add the applesauce and cinnamon and process until a dough begins to form, about 30 seconds. Transfer to a clean bowl. The mixture will be moist.

If your granola is very clumpy, add it to the food processor and process until it breaks down to pea-size pieces, about 10 seconds. Be sure not to overprocess, as you don't want a powdery consistency; a mixture of fine and medium pieces is good. If your granola already looks like this, skip this step. Transfer to a bowl and set aside.

Using your hands, evenly mix ¾ cup of the granola into the dough. Roll the dough into 1-inch balls (see box, page 34). Place on the prepared cookie sheet and refrigerate uncovered for 45 minutes.

While the balls are in the refrigerator, melt and temper the white chocolate (or melt Wilton Candy Melts). Dip each ball into the white chocolate, and return to the prepared cookie sheet. Sprinkle all with the remaining ¼ cup granola. Refrigerate until solid, about 1 hour.

coo coo for coconut

I LOVE THIS TRUFFLE BECAUSE *it has a really strong coconut flavor without giving you the instant toothache that most coconut treats give you. The graininess of the graham crackers and bitterness of the dark chocolate cut the sweetness of the coconut and honey down to just the right amount. I love serving these in the summer. Toasted coconut* always *goes great with the sun.*

◇◇◇◇◇◇◇◇◇◇◇◇◇**MAKES ABOUT 20 TREATS**◇◇◇◇◇◇◇◇◇◇◇◇◇

Line a cookie sheet with wax paper and set aside.

In a food processor, process the graham crackers until fine crumbs form, about 1 minute. Add the chocolate chips and a little more than half of the coconut flakes and process for about 20 seconds, until the mixture is evenly distributed. Add the honey, cream cheese, and coconut oil and process until thoroughly combined, about 30 seconds. Transfer to a clean bowl.

Press the mixture together with your hands to form a dough. Roll the dough into 1-inch balls (see box, page 34). Place on the prepared cookie sheet and refrigerate uncovered for 45 minutes.

Place the butter in a small sauté pan over medium heat and heat until barely melted, about 30 seconds. Add the remaining coconut flakes and sauté until golden brown, stirring constantly, about 2 minutes. Transfer to a small bowl.

Melt and temper the chocolate (or melt Wilton Candy Melts).

Remove the balls from the refrigerator. Dip each ball into the chocolate, return it to the prepared cookie sheet, and sprinkle with the crunchy coconut flakes. Refrigerate until solid, about 1 hour.

6 standard graham cracker sheets, broken into pieces

1 tablespoon dark chocolate chips

½ cup coconut flakes, sweetened

2 tablespoons honey

1 tablespoon cream cheese, softened (I recommend using light or ⅓ fat)

1½ tablespoons coconut oil

1 teaspoon unsalted butter

1½ cups dark chocolate chopped into quarter-size pieces (or Wilton Candy Melts)

fruity two-bite

EVERY YEAR FOR VALENTINE'S DAY, *whether my husband and I go out for a prix-fixe dinner or stay in and enjoy takeout and a movie, I make him some kind of goodie. These truffles are his all-time favorite, and they are a creative alternative to the overdone chocolate-covered strawberry. Plus, sometimes the dried strawberry toppers look like little hearts, especially after some bubbly!*

MAKES ABOUT 25 TREATS

20 shortbread cookies (small square ones work well—I like Lorna Doone)

¼ cup heavy cream

¼ cup strawberry jam (seedless and without fruit pieces)

1 cup white chocolate chopped into quarter-size pieces (or Wilton Candy Melts)

3 tablespoons unsalted butter

1 cup dried strawberries

I recommend using a cookie scoop or melon baller to measure out your dough before rolling it into a perfectly shaped truffle with your hands. This technique will give you a head start in making your treat the right shape and size. It applies to almost all the treats in this chapter and will come in very handy when we get to mini pies as well.

Line an 8 by 8-inch baking pan with plastic wrap and set aside.

Process the cookies in a food processor until fine crumbs form, about 30 seconds. Transfer to a clean bowl and set aside. You should have about 1 cup of cookie crumbs.

Pour the cream into a small nonstick saucepan; place over medium heat and heat until the cream comes to a low boil, about 1 minute. Turn the heat down to a simmer and stir in the jam until melted.

Melt 2 tablespoons of the white chocolate in the microwave on high power, about 1 minute. Remove the saucepan from the heat and, using a whisk, mix the melted chocolate and the butter into the cream-jam mixture until completely combined. Add the cookie crumbs to the mixture and stir well to create a dough. Pour the dough into the prepared pan and cover with plastic wrap. Refrigerate for 2 hours.

Line a cookie sheet with wax paper and set aside.

Roll the refrigerated dough into 1-inch balls (see box). Place on the prepared cookie sheet and return to the refrigerator for 1 hour.

Melt and temper the remaining white chocolate (or melt Wilton Candy Melts). Dip each ball into the melted white chocolate, place back on the prepared cookie sheet, and top with a dried strawberry. Refrigerate until solid, about 1 hour.

bite o' joe

I HAVE TO CONFESS, I am a total coffee addict. No matter what I am making or what time of day it is, I always have a cup of coffee by my side in the kitchen. I must have picked it up from my mother—she does it too. My sister gifted her with a heated coffee coaster for Christmas a couple of years ago—how genius. She loved it…and I was kind of jealous! I came up with this treat while I was making a vanilla wafer crust for a fruit tart—with my coffee, of course, in hand. I impulsively poured a little coffee into the cookie crumbs, mixed it up, and boom, Bite o' Joe was born.

⬥⬥⬥⬥⬥⬥⬥⬥⬥⬥⬥⬥⬥⬥ MAKES ABOUT 20 TREATS ⬥⬥⬥⬥⬥⬥⬥⬥⬥⬥⬥⬥⬥⬥

Line a cookie sheet with wax paper and set aside.

In a coffee cup, stir the allspice into the hot espresso to bloom the spice.

Process the wafers in a food processor until fine crumbs form, about 1 minute. Add the espresso mixture, half-and-half, and salt and process until a dough begins to form, about 30 seconds. Transfer the dough to a clean bowl.

Roll the mixture into 1-inch balls (see box, page 34) and place on the prepared cookie sheet. Refrigerate uncovered for 45 minutes.

Melt and temper the white chocolate (or melt Wilton Candy Melts). Dip each ball into the white chocolate, return to the cookie sheet, and top with a single espresso bean. Refrigerate for 1 hour, or until solid.

¾ teaspoon ground allspice

¼ cup hot brewed espresso

60 vanilla wafers (I like Nilla Wafers because the reduced-fat version tastes great!)

¼ cup half-and-half

Pinch of salt

1½ cups white chocolate chopped into quarter-size pieces (or Wilton Candy Melts)

¼ cup espresso beans

Similar to the way garlic, red pepper, or even rosemary is infused into olive oil to enhance its flavor in a savory dish, adding allspice to the espresso in this recipe releases the oils and boosts the taste, helping to give this truffle an extra kick.

cinni minni

EVERY SATURDAY AND SUNDAY *the bakery down our street, Champs, makes the most delicious cinnamon rolls. We can smell them baking from a block away. The only problem? They are insanely enormous. Unless you are using one as a birthday cake (which I actually did for my husband's surprise birthday party a couple of years ago), they are so big that even sharing among two or three people results in a shame-walk home. But they are inspiring: I like to think of these truffles as their tiny, no bake baby sister. They are cinni and mini and definitely a winni. (Yes, that's an abbreviation for winner.)*

◇◇◇◇◇◇◇◇◇◇◇◇◇◇◇◇◇**MAKES ABOUT 25 TREATS**◇◇◇◇◇◇◇◇◇◇◇◇◇◇◇◇◇

Line a cookie sheet with wax paper and set aside.

In a food processor, process the cookies until fine crumbs form, about 1 minute. Add the raisins, brown sugar, and 1½ teaspoons of the cinnamon and process for another 30 seconds.

Whisk together the sweetened condensed milk, softened butter, vanilla, and milk in a small bowl until smooth. Pour evenly over the vanilla wafer mixture and mix until a dough begins to form, about 30 seconds. Transfer the dough to a clean bowl.

Roll the dough into 1-inch balls (see box, page 34) and place on the prepared pan.

Prepare the chocolate for drizzling. Drizzle each truffle with milk chocolate and sprinkle with the remaining 1 teaspoon cinnamon. Refrigerate for 30 minutes or until solid and serve.

60 vanilla wafers (I like Nilla Wafers)

⅓ cup seedless raisins

3 teaspoons firmly packed brown sugar

3 teaspoons ground cinnamon

3 tablespoons sweetened condensed milk

1½ tablespoons unsalted butter, softened

¾ teaspoon vanilla extract

1½ tablespoons skim milk

½ cup milk chocolate chopped into quarter-size pieces (or Wilton Candy Melts)

the clary

24 shortbread cookies (small square ones work well—I like Lorna Doone)

6 tablespoons guava paste, at room temperature

2 tablespoons cream cheese, softened (I recommend light or ⅓ fat)

¼ cup powdered sugar

MY AUNT CLARY, *the family's designated worrywart, sent me a care package after Tropical Storm Irene in New York. We take near hurricanes very seriously in Miami, but I assured her several times that I was entirely safe and it was just some wind and a whole lot of rain. Convinced that I had suffered some kind of real weather trauma, Aunt Clary sent along some classically Cuban comfort foods, including guava paste, which is traditionally spread on Cuban crackers with cream cheese. With that yummy snack in mind, I took it a few steps further and made this guava cookie truffle. Now every time I make it, I think about how caring my aunt Clary is.*

MAKES ABOUT 20 TREATS

Line a cookie sheet with wax paper and set aside.

Process the cookies in a food processor until fine crumbs form, about 1 minute. Add 3 tablespoons of the guava paste and the cream cheese and process until a dough begins to form, about 30 seconds. Transfer the dough to a clean bowl.

Roll the dough into 1-inch balls (see box, page 34). Place on the prepared cookie sheet and refrigerate uncovered for 45 minutes.

As if you were preparing to drizzle chocolate, spoon the remaining guava paste into the corner of a sandwich bag and dip the corner into hot water until the guava paste melts, about 1 minute. Remove the balls from the refrigerator and cut off the very tip of the corner of the bag. Squeeze a swirl of guava onto each bite to decorate. Sift powdered sugar over the truffles.

try using

nonmelting powdered sugar (I like King Arthur Flour brand) to sift over the truffles. This technique is great for donuts, crepes, or anything you'd like to sprinkle with a little extra sweetness. Using this kind of powdered sugar allows you to sift the sugar on ahead of time, knowing it will stay bright white and unmelted on top of your treats for several days.

maple pecan bite

COOKIES AND CREAM MIXED WITH *maple syrup is no joke. When these two powerhouses combine, they form the most heavenly and sinful bite ever. Add in a little cinnamon and some pecans, and it's like the best tiny piece of pecan pie you've ever tasted. For extra decadence, serve these with hot syrup on the side!*

×◇×◇×◇×◇×◇×◇×◇×◇**MAKES ABOUT 20 TREATS**×◇×◇×◇×◇×◇×◇×◇×◇

Line a cookie sheet with wax paper and set aside.

Pulse the pecans in a food processor until pea-size, about 15 seconds. Transfer to a bowl and set aside. Add the cookies to the food processor and process until fine crumbs form, about 1 minute. Pour the maple syrup over the cookie crumbs, add 1 teaspoon of the cinnamon and the cream cheese, and mix until a dough begins to form, about 30 seconds. Transfer the dough to a clean bowl.

Mix the pecans into the dough using your hands until they are evenly distributed. Roll the dough into 1-inch balls (see box, page 34). Place on the prepared cookie sheet and refrigerate uncovered for 45 minutes.

Sift the remaining ½ teaspoon cinnamon and the powdered sugar onto the truffles to decorate (see box, page 41).

½ cup roasted salted pecans

15 vanilla sandwich cookies (Joe-Joes are my favorite)

1½ tablespoons maple syrup

1½ teaspoons ground cinnamon

2 tablespoons cream cheese, softened (I recommend light or ⅓ fat)

2 tablespoons powdered sugar

National Maple Syrup Day is December 17. What better way to celebrate?

chocolate chip cookie remix

15 store-bought chocolate chip cookies (I like Chips Ahoy or Keebler)

2 tablespoons honey

2 tablespoons cream cheese, softened (I recommend using light or ⅓ fat)

1½ cups white chocolate chopped into quarter-size pieces (or Wilton Candy Melts)

¾ cup milk or dark mini chocolate chips

THIS ONE GOES OUT TO *my big brother Toti: the ultimate fan of "kinda-hard-but-awesomely-milk-dippable" store-bought chocolate chip cookies. My mom still puts them in the cookie jar when he goes to her house (he's in his thirties). While I don't share the same enthusiasm for these cookies in their original form, they make a fantastic dry agent for this remix truffle. Their shape may not be as convenient for milk dipping, but it can be done if need be...think fork.*

MAKES ABOUT 20 TREATS

Line a cookie sheet with wax paper and set aside.

Process the cookies in a food processor until fine crumbs form, about 1 minute. Add the honey and cream cheese and process until a dough begins to form, about 30 seconds. Transfer the dough to a clean bowl.

Roll the dough into 1-inch balls (see box, page 34). Place on the prepared cookie sheet and refrigerate uncovered for 45 minutes.

Melt and temper the white chocolate (or melt Wilton Candy Melts). Dip each ball into the white chocolate, return to the cookie sheet, and sprinkle with the mini chocolate chips. Refrigerate for 1 hour, or until solid.

booze balls

THESE ARE VERY BOOZY. So boozy that I recommend you let them sit in the refrigerator for a minimum of 48 hours to allow the flavors to settle a bit. The sting from the bourbon mixed with the richness of the chocolate is a perfect combination. It's just what the doctor ordered for the holidays.

MAKES ABOUT 20 TREATS

7 standard graham cracker sheets

¾ cup dark chocolate chopped into quarter-size pieces (or Wilton Candy Melts)

¼ cup granulated sugar

1½ tablespoons light corn syrup

¼ cup bourbon

3 tablespoons cocoa powder

3 tablespoons crystallized sugar (choose your favorite color)

Line a cookie sheet with wax paper and set aside.

Process the graham crackers in a food processor until fine crumbs form, about 30 seconds. Set aside.

Heat the chocolate in the microwave in 15-second intervals until melted and pour it into a large bowl. Using a spatula, stir in the granulated sugar and corn syrup. Add the bourbon and continue to stir. Add the graham cracker crumbs and mix until evenly distributed. Cover and refrigerate for about 45 minutes.

Mix the cocoa powder and crystallized sugar together in a small bowl.

Roll the mixture into 1-inch truffles (see box, page 34); then dip into the cocoa powder–sugar mixture and place on the prepared cookie sheet. Let the treats sit in the refrigerator for at least 48 hours. Top with more cocoa powder and crystallized sugar just before serving.

the cookie union

8 store-bought chocolate chip cookies (I like Keebler or Chips Ahoy)

8 chocolate sandwich cookies (I like Joe-Joes)

2 tablespoons honey

2 tablespoons marshmallow fluff

1 tablespoon salted creamy peanut butter

1½ cups milk chocolate chopped into quarter-size pieces (or Wilton Candy Melts)

¼ cup peanut butter chips

WHEN WE WERE KIDS, *my cousin and I used to peel the tops off Oreos, add peanut butter and fluff to the cream center, and put a chocolate chip cookie on top. Pretty inventive, right? Proud of our own genius, we named it "The Most Yummy Dessert Sandwich!" The creation is of course still yummy, but just a little too messy to serve at a grown-up gathering. The Cookie Union is the convenient, upgraded, and still totally delicious version of our tasty childhood treat.*

◇◇◇◇◇◇◇◇◇◇MAKES ABOUT 20 TREATS◇◇◇◇◇◇◇◇◇◇◇◇◇

Line a cookie sheet with wax paper and set aside.

Process the chocolate chip cookies and chocolate sandwich cookies in a food processor until fine crumbs form, about 1 minute. Scoop out about a tablespoon of crumbs and set aside for garnish. Add the honey, fluff, and peanut butter and mix until a dough begins to form, about 30 seconds. Transfer the dough to a clean bowl.

Roll the dough into 1-inch balls (see box, page 34). Place on the prepared cookie sheet. Refrigerate uncovered for 45 minutes.

Melt and temper the chocolate (or melt Wilton Candy Melts). Dip each ball into the melted chocolate, return to the cookie sheet, and garnish with the crumbs and peanut butter chips. Refrigerate for 30 minutes, or until solid.

minty

THIN MINTS ARE CONSISTENTLY THE *number one top-selling cookie for the Girl Scouts of America. They're so addictive and delicious—it's not hard to see why! Since so many of us wait patiently all year to get our hands on them during Girl Scout cookie season, I wanted to create an opportunity to do more with them. In the Minty truffle, I've plumped them up a bit to, dare I say, improve them. If you like Thin Mints, you will love Minty! She's a little more decadent and a lot more fun. Looking to earn a new Girl Scout badge? Look no further.*

◇◇◇◇◇◇◇◇◇◇◇◇◇◇◇**MAKES ABOUT 20 TREATS**◇◇◇◇◇◇◇◇◇◇◇◇◇

Line a cookie sheet with wax paper and set aside.

Process the cookies and mint cream–filled candies in a food processor until pea-size crumbs form, about 1 minute. Add the coconut oil and process until a dough begins to form, about 30 seconds. Transfer the dough to a clean bowl. Refrigerate uncovered for 30 minutes.

Roll the dough into 1-inch balls (see box, page 34). Place on the prepared cookie sheet. Refrigerate for another 30 minutes.

Melt and temper the chocolate (or melt Wilton Candy Melts). Dip the truffles into the melted dark chocolate, return to the cookie sheet, and sprinkle with the chopped mint chocolate pieces. Refrigerate for 20 minutes, or until solid.

24 mint cookies (I like Thin Mints, but store-brand versions are available year-round)

2 large chocolate mint cream–filled candies, at room temperature (I like York Peppermint Patties)

3 tablespoons coconut oil

1½ cups dark chocolate chopped into quarter-size pieces (or Wilton Candy Melts)

½ cup finely chopped mint chocolate pieces (I like Andes candies)

Clusters
AND
Bark

Sweet & Salty

Honeysweets

Sweechies

Chex This Out

Captain Yum

Cherry Bomb

Peanut Brittle

Cinnamon & Spice

The Mama

Nutty for Apricot

Buckeye Bark

Whiskey Me Away

S'mores

Clusters are yummy
Bark is quick
Anyone can make them
As long as the chocolate is slick
Just mix in your fave cereal, nuts, and more
Break up your bites and you'll have treats galore!

Every recipe in this chapter is quick to make and a definite crowd-pleaser. And most of them work really well as gifts. Just break up your bark or clusters and place them in a glass jar. Tie a ribbon around the jar and kiss your holiday gift-giving or hostess stress away.

Right after college, while I was looking for my first "real career" job, I was working two part-time jobs. Half the week I worked as a sales associate at the clothing shop in the Equinox gym. I can say with confidence that I have a pretty awesome workout wardrobe as a result. The other half, I temped at an advertising agency where my main task was to input numbers from a printed spreadsheet to an electronic one. It wasn't fun. Long story short: I had no time, even less money, and an unusual amount of "work friends" to give holiday gifts to that year. The solution? Bark and clusters.

I shared a basket of these treats in the Equinox staff kitchen and gained major points with the trainers, who, despite their fit physiques, I knew would love a sweet snack. At the ad agency, I gave out individual jars of them to the execs. A couple of months later, I was offered a permanent job there (which I declined). Coincidence? I think not.

sweet & salty

I'VE NEVER BEEN A HUGE pumpkin pie or bread pudding fan, so for years I've contributed to my family's Thanksgiving dinner by making a dessert that doesn't fall into a typical Thanksgiving dessert category. Of course, when the time was right, I decided to no bake these Sweet & Salties to show off my new business endeavor. My Cuban grandmother was a bit confused when I told her I did not need the oven preheated. I remember telling her I was making clusters, then hearing the response in her thick Hispanic accent: "cloosters?" I replied that they were "sweet and salty things." Abuela ended up eating a bunch. Delicioso!

◇◇◇◇◇◇◇◇◇◇◇◇◇◇◇◇◇**MAKES ABOUT 40 TREATS**◇◇◇◇◇◇◇◇◇◇◇◇◇◇◇

1½ cups chocolate puffed grain breakfast cereal (I like Cocoa Puffs)

1½ cups salted peanuts

1½ cups milk chocolate chopped into quarter-size pieces (or Wilton Candy Melts)

1 tablespoon sea salt

Line a 9 by 13-inch baking pan with aluminum foil and coat it with nonstick spray. Set aside.

Mix the cereal and peanuts in a large bowl until evenly distributed.

Melt and temper the chocolate (or melt Wilton Candy Melts). Pour the chocolate over the cereal mixture and, using a rubber spatula, stir until the cereal and nuts are completely coated.

Use the spatula to spread the mixture evenly over the bottom of the prepared pan. Sprinkle with the salt. Refrigerate for 1 hour, or until solid. Break or cut into two-bite pieces.

When making clusters and bark, specifically those that are layered, such as Honeysweets (page 56), Cinnamon & Spice (page 68), and S'mores (page 79), you'll find that you'll make much cleaner cuts if you run your knife under very hot water and dry it thoroughly before cutting your bark or clusters. A warm knife makes cutting much easier. Otherwise, the chocolate may snap in the wrong direction or a layer may pop off. That said, you can always use your hands to break it up if you feel like it!

honeysweets

1 cup butterscotch chips

1 cup Honey Nut Cheerios

1 cup roughly chopped pecans

2 tablespoons honey

1½ cups white chocolate chopped into quarter-size pieces (or Wilton Candy Melts)

I DO AN ODD THING *with my Cheerios: I buy the plain ones, then honey and nut them myself. Before pouring milk over them, I add chopped pecans and a drizzle of honey to the bowl. Why not turn this delight into a two-bite treat? Since we want our dessert just a little sweeter than breakfast, I opted for the Honey Nut version as the base of the bark—but of course we're still adding a little more honey and a lot more nuts to seal the deal!*

MAKES ABOUT 40 TREATS

Line a 9 by 13-inch baking pan with aluminum foil and coat it with nonstick spray. Set aside.

Melt the butterscotch chips in the microwave on high in 15-second intervals (3 or 4 intervals), stirring after each interval, until smooth. Using a rubber spatula, spread the mixture evenly along the bottom of the prepared pan. Refrigerate for 10 minutes.

Mix the cereal, nuts, and honey in a large bowl until evenly distributed.

Melt and temper the white chocolate (or melt Wilton Candy Melts). Pour the white chocolate over the dry mixture and stir until the cereal and nuts are completely coated.

Using a rubber spatula, spread the white chocolate–coated mixture evenly over the butterscotch layer in the pan. Refrigerate for 1 hour, or until solid. Break or cut into two-bite pieces.

sweechies

TO CELEBRATE EASTER, *my whole family in Miami gets together for an enormous brunch. When I couldn't travel down there one year, I was bummed and missing family, so I tried my best to mimic the tradition with an oven-baked honey-glazed ham and cheesy egg frittata. With the oven clearly occupied, I quickly whipped up this sweet and crunchy bark for dessert. It added such a happy and festive element to what I'm happy to say is my and my husband's new Easter tradition.*

◇◇◇◇◇◇◇◇◇◇◇◇◇◇**MAKES ABOUT 40 TREATS**◇◇◇◇◇◇◇◇◇◇◇◇◇◇

Line a 9 by 13-inch baking pan with aluminum foil and coat it with nonstick spray. Set aside.

Place the cereal and coconut flakes in a large bowl and stir until distributed evenly.

Melt and temper the white chocolate. Pour the white chocolate over the mixture and stir until completely coated. Using a rubber spatula, spread the mixture evenly over the bottom of the prepared pan. Sprinkle with sprinkles!

Refrigerate for 30 minutes, or until solid. Transfer to a cutting board, peel off the foil, and cut with a very sharp knife or break into two-bite pieces.

1½ cups fruity cereal (I like Fruity Pebbles)

1½ cups coconut flakes

2½ cups white chocolate chopped into quarter-size pieces (or Wilton Candy Melts)

½ cup sprinkles of your choice

Betty Crocker makes the cutest, most colorful Easter sprinkles, complete with little white edible bunny ears! They're my favorite when I'm making Sweechies for Easter.

chex this out

A FEW YEARS AGO I *went through a serious Chex phase, adding them to both sweet and savory foods, creating an impressive, if I do say so myself, repertoire of trail mixes. After a while, I exhausted that avenue but found a new use for the cereal staple: Chex makes a great base for clusters. This is where they really shine. They are crunchy and light, and their little holes make a perfect gateway for chocolate.*

MAKES ABOUT 40 TREATS

Line a 9 by 13-inch baking pan with aluminum foil and coat it with nonstick spray. Set aside.

Combine the cereal, pretzels, and cinnamon in a large bowl.

Melt and temper the white chocolate (or melt Wilton Candy Melts). Pour the white chocolate evenly over the mixture and stir until distributed evenly.

Using a rubber spatula, spread the mixture evenly over the bottom of the prepared pan. Refrigerate for 30 minutes, or until solid. Transfer to a cutting board. Break or cut with a sharp knife into two-bite pieces.

2 cups plain Chex cereal

1 cup roughly chopped or broken salted pretzels

2 teaspoons ground cinnamon

1½ cups white chocolate chopped into quarter-size pieces (or Wilton Candy Melts)

captain yum

2 cups crunchy corn cereal (I like Cap'n Crunch)

1 cup chopped walnuts

1½ cups milk chocolate chopped into quarter-size pieces (or Wilton Candy Melts)

DURING MY FRESHMAN YEAR *of college I shared a tiny dorm room with my friend Lorelle—our beds were literally two feet away from each other. I would always hear crunch, crunch, crunching coming from the other bed! When I looked over, there was Lorelle, digging her hand into a fresh box of Cap'n Crunch. The noise drove me crazy—but I would inevitably ask her for a handful every time. She'd close up the bag, secure the box, and throw it across to me. I'd take my share and throw it right back. And so it continued. While these Captain Yum clusters do not involve throwing, they are just as addictive as eating cereal out of a box.*

MAKES ABOUT 40 TREATS

Line a 9 by 13-inch baking sheet with aluminum foil and coat it with nonstick spray. Set aside.

Combine the cereal and walnuts in a large bowl.

Melt and temper the chocolate (or melt Wilton Candy Melts). Pour the chocolate evenly over the mixture and stir until distributed evenly.

Using a rubber spatula, spread the mixture evenly over the bottom of the prepared pan. Refrigerate for 30 minutes, or until totally solid. Break or cut into two-bite pieces.

cherry bomb

IT'S NO SECRET *that dark chocolate has tons of antioxidants. Health mags and blogs always tell us to keep some squares of dark chocolate in the freezer to curb sugar cravings. For me, a square of dark chocolate doesn't quite cut it, so I upped the ante. Not only will adding dried cherries and almonds to your chocolate make your treat even sweeter, but their vitamin E antioxidants, flavonoids, monounsaturated fat, and fiber will also help prevent heart disease and improve your sleep patterns.*

1½ cups sliced almonds

1½ cups dried cherries

1½ cups dark chocolate chopped into quarter-size pieces (or Wilton Candy Melts)

◇◇◇◇◇◇◇◇◇◇◇◇◇◇◇◇MAKES ABOUT 40 TREATS◇◇◇◇◇◇◇◇◇◇◇◇◇◇◇◇

Line a 9 by 13-inch baking sheet with aluminum foil and coat it with nonstick spray. Set aside.

Combine 1 cup of the almonds and 1 cup of the cherries in a large bowl.

Melt and temper the dark chocolate (or melt Wilton Candy Melts). Pour the chocolate evenly over the mixture and stir until distributed evenly.

Using a rubber spatula, spread the mixture evenly over the bottom of the prepared pan. Sprinkle with the remaining ½ cup almonds and ½ cup cherries. Refrigerate for 30 minutes, or until totally solid. Break or cut into two-bite pieces using a very sharp knife.

peanut brittle

3 cups roasted salted peanuts

2 cups granulated sugar

1 cup light corn syrup

2 tablespoons unsalted butter

2 teaspoons vanilla extract

2 teaspoons baking soda

2 teaspoons coarse sea salt
(optional)

Be very, very careful when making this treat. Melted sugar can burn you easily. The mixture gets mega-hot.

IN GRADE SCHOOL DURING THE HOLIDAYS, we were given fund-raising catalogs that offered everything from gift wrap to Santa Claus key chains. Students would have a couple of weeks to solicit their families and neighbors to place orders (you remember these, right?). My grandmother, my best customer, always ordered the same thing: peanut brittle in a festive tin. I loved how long it lasted because it was so chewy. It seemed like a mysterious treat at the time—such an interesting combination of sweet and salty, smooth and hard. Little did I know how easy it was to make! We still enjoy this treat, even though the days of those catalogs are long gone.

◇◇◇◇◇◇◇◇◇◇◇◇◇◇◇◇◇◇◇◇ MAKES ABOUT 40 TREATS ◇◇◇◇◇◇◇◇◇◇◇◇◇◇◇◇◇◇◇◇

Line a 9 by 13-inch baking pan with aluminum foil and coat it with nonstick spray. Set aside.

In a large microwave-safe bowl, combine the peanuts, sugar, and corn syrup and stir well with a rubber spatula. Microwave for 7 to 8 minutes on high power, until the mixture is bubbly and the peanuts are browned. Stir in the butter and vanilla—it will sizzle and pop! Place back in the microwave on high until very bubbly, 1 to 2 minutes.

Quickly stir in the baking soda just until the mixture is foamy. Immediately pour into the prepared pan and sprinkle with the salt.

Let cool at room temperature for 20 minutes, or until firm. Break into two-bite pieces.

cinnamon & spice

1½ cups dark chocolate chopped into quarter-size pieces (or Wilton Candy Melts)

1½ teaspoons ground cayenne

1½ cups white chocolate chopped into quarter-size pieces (or Wilton Candy Melts)

½ teaspoon ground cinnamon

1 cup roughly chopped salted pecans

THIS IS A BARK WITH *some bite! You'll definitely want to have some milk handy when you eat this spicy bark. Just a taste of it will make you say "Ayayay!" My husband always complains that I make our dinners too spicy. What can I say? My hands become a little wiggly around cayenne pepper. With that said, it is no surprise that this is one of my favorite bark recipes by far.*

◇◇◇◇◇◇◇◇◇◇◇◇◇◇◇◇◇◇◇**MAKES ABOUT 40 TREATS**◇◇◇◇◇◇◇◇◇◇◇◇◇◇◇◇◇◇◇

Line a 9 by 13-inch baking pan with aluminum foil and coat it with nonstick spray. Set aside.

Melt and temper the dark chocolate (or melt Wilton Candy Melts). Add 1 teaspoon of the cayenne to the melted dark chocolate and mix well.

Using a rubber spatula, spread the mixture evenly over the bottom of the prepared pan. Refrigerate for 30 minutes, or until completely solid.

Melt and temper the white chocolate (or melt Wilton Candy Melts). Add the cinnamon and the remaining ½ teaspoon cayenne to the melted white chocolate and mix well. Pour the white chocolate over the dark chocolate layer and smooth out evenly with a spatula.

Sprinkle the pecans evenly over the bark and refrigerate for another 30 minutes, or until solid. Break or cut into two-bite pieces.

the mama

WHEN I FIRST CALLED MY MOM *to let her know I was writing a cookbook, she was beyond thrilled. We immediately started brainstorming recipe ideas. The very first thing she said was, "Well, to start off, anything mixed with raisins is good." So simple and so true. This one's for you, Mama!*

MAKES ABOUT 40 TREATS

Line a 9 by 13-inch baking pan with aluminum foil and coat it with nonstick spray. Set aside.

Melt and temper the milk chocolate (or melt Wilton Candy Melts). Pour the chocolate evenly over the bottom of the prepared pan. Sprinkle with ½ teaspoon of the salt. Refrigerate for 30 minutes, or until solid.

Melt and temper the dark chocolate (or melt Wilton Candy Melts). Mix in the raisins and spread the mixture evenly over the milk chocolate layer. Sprinkle with the remaining ½ teaspoon salt.

Refrigerate for about 30 minutes, until solid. Break or cut into two-bite pieces.

1½ cups milk chocolate chopped into quarter-size pieces (or Wilton Candy Melts)

1 teaspoon sea salt

1½ cups dark chocolate chopped into quarter-size pieces (or Wilton Candy Melts)

1½ cups raisins

nutty for apricot

1 cup finely chopped dried apricots

1 cup unsalted sliced almonds

2 cups white chocolate chopped into quarter-size pieces (or Wilton Candy Melts)

1½ teaspoons ground nutmeg

ON A RECENT TRIP TO ITALY, *we visited my friend Steph's parents, who live in an absolutely breathtaking villa overlooking Florence. Among the many reasons the visit was lovely was the freshly made apricot jam we spread on crackers alongside our coffee. The apricots were picked right from a tree on their property; the jam was so naturally sweet and tart at the same time. It gave me a new appreciation for this under-the-radar fruit.*

MAKES ABOUT 40 TREATS

Line a 9 by 13-inch baking pan with aluminum foil and coat it with nonstick spray. Set aside.

Combine the apricots and almonds in a large bowl.

Melt and temper the white chocolate (or melt Wilton Candy Melts). Stir the nutmeg into the melted chocolate. Pour over the apricot-nut mixture and stir until distributed evenly.

Using a rubber spatula, spread the mixture evenly over the bottom of the prepared pan. Refrigerate for 30 minutes, or until solid. Break or cut into two-bite pieces.

buckeye bark

THE ORIGINAL BUCKEYE CANDY *is a truffle that came out of Ohio, the Buckeye State. The candy is meant to resemble the nut of the buckeye tree. The smooth peanut butter filling makes them incredibly delicious. But since my kitchen is in Brooklyn and we have no attachment to the origin, I decided to do things a little differently by upping the peanut butter ratio and spreading it into a bark. And it's even better, if I do say so myself.*

◇◇◇◇◇◇◇◇◇◇◇◇◇◇◇◇◇**MAKES ABOUT 40 TREATS**◇◇◇◇◇◇◇◇◇◇◇◇◇◇◇◇◇

1½ cups dark chocolate chopped into quarter-size pieces (or Wilton Candy Melts)

¾ cup salted creamy peanut butter

½ cup (1 stick) unsalted butter, softened

¼ teaspoon vanilla extract

2 cups powdered sugar, sifted

1 cup white chocolate cut into small pieces

Line a 9 by 13-inch baking pan with aluminum foil and coat it with nonstick spray. Set aside.

Melt and temper the dark chocolate and pour it into the prepared pan. Use a rubber spatula to spread it evenly. Refrigerate for 30 minutes, or until solid.

Combine the peanut butter, butter, vanilla, and powdered sugar in a large bowl and whisk until smooth. Spread over the chocolate layer in the pan and return to the refrigerator for 30 minutes.

Meanwhile, prepare the white chocolate for drizzling. Drizzle the white chocolate on top of the peanut butter layer. Return to the refrigerator for 30 minutes, or until solid. Cut (don't break this one) into two-bite pieces.

Peanut butter and almond butter are naturally gluten-free, but when they come in contact with a knife that has touched wheat bread, they become contaminated. If your household is not gluten-free but you are entertaining a gluten-free guest, be sure to get a new jar before you make your recipe. It's a common (and easy to miss!) cross-contamination mistake.

whiskey me away

YOU'LL NEVER FIND ANOTHER RECIPE *where Cinnamon Toast Crunch and whiskey meet. The ingredient list may make it seem like a tornado went through my pantry (and my liquor cabinet) to create this bite, but don't let that scare you away—it's worth your while. The crunchy cereal is a great foundation for the bitter, sweet, and boozy flavors. It may be a little crazy, but it's a lot delicious.*

◇◇◇◇◇◇◇◇◇◇◇◇◇◇**MAKES ABOUT 40 TREATS**◇◇◇◇◇◇◇◇◇◇◇◇◇◇

Line a 9 by 13-inch baking pan with aluminum foil and coat it with nonstick spray. Set aside.

Pour 2 cups of the cereal into the pan to create an even layer.

Melt and temper the dark chocolate (or melt Wilton Candy Melts) and pour into a large bowl. Add the peanut butter and mix until smooth. Pour half of the mixture (about 1 cup) over the cereal, using a rubber spatula to spread it. Add the remaining cereal as the next layer. Next, pour in the remaining peanut butter–chocolate mixture and smooth it out with a spatula.

Heat the butterscotch chips in the microwave on high power in 15-second intervals until melted, stirring after each interval, about 1 minute total. Stir the whiskey into the melted butterscotch. Pour the mixture over the dark chocolate layer in the pan. Use a fork to swirl around the butterscotch mixture, creating your own funky pattern.

Let sit at room temperature for about 10 minutes; then refrigerate for 45 minutes, or until solid.

Remove the block from the pan and transfer it to a cutting board. Peel off the foil and cut (don't break this one) into 1 by 1-inch squares with a very sharp knife.

4 cups Cinnamon Toast Crunch cereal

2 cups dark chocolate chopped into quarter-size pieces (or Wilton Candy Melts)

½ cup salted creamy peanut butter

⅔ cup butterscotch chips

⅛ cup whiskey (add more to taste)

Need some fun design inspiration? To make a swirly pattern, make semicircles with your fork, alternating the direction. To make a plaid effect, run your fork straight across the pan in both directions. Use your imagination! No matter the look, the taste will always be yummy.

s'mores

DID YOU KNOW THAT S'MORE *is short for "some more"? I know. It seems so obvious now! It's no surprise that the name stuck with a graham cracker, marshmallow, and chocolate sandwich treat. Since there really isn't a time that you don't want some more of this never-to-be-messed-with flavor combination, I created a bark you can make anytime—no campfire required!*

◇◇◇◇◇◇◇◇◇◇◇◇**MAKES ABOUT 40 TREATS**◇◇◇◇◇◇◇◇◇◇◇◇

Line a 9 by 13-inch baking pan with aluminum foil and coat it with nonstick spray. Set aside.

Place 2 graham cracker sheets in a zip-top bag, seal it, and crush them into crumbs using your hands. Set aside.

Melt and temper the chocolate (or melt Wilton Candy Melts). Pour 1 cup of the chocolate into the prepared pan and use a rubber spatula to spread it evenly. Allow to sit at room temperature for 10 minutes. Place 8 full graham cracker sheets across the chocolate layer. Pour the remaining melted chocolate over the graham cracker layer and spread evenly with a spatula.

Sprinkle with the mini marshmallows and the graham cracker crumbs. Refrigerate for 45 minutes, or until solid.

Transfer to a cutting board and peel off the foil. Break or cut into two-bite pieces.

10 standard graham
cracker sheets

2½ cups milk or dark chocolate
chopped into quarter-size pieces
(or Wilton Candy Melts)

1 cup mini marshmallows

When it comes time to crush the graham crackers in the zip-top bag, hand it over to your kids. Kids do a great job and absolutely love this step!

Fudge

AND

Bars

Beary Surprise

PB&Ps

Danger Squares

Banana Crunch Bars

Pecamel Fudgey Bars

Marshmallow Pretzel Bars

Layers o' Mint

Almond Butter Fudge

The Sadie

The Sebi

There are certain recipes that people tend to stay away from because they can get a little sloppy. Fudge, for example, gets a bad rap. Yes, it can be a mess, but only because its ingredients are gooey and decadent. But doesn't that only make it better?

Every recipe in this chapter has what I call the "lick your fingers" quality. These bites aren't the clean and simple type. Some of the bars have creamy toppings, some have a sticky marshmallow consistency, others have layers of crunch, and several have crumble. But what they all have in common is that you'll have to—and want to—lick your fingers when they're all gone. *That's* the secret ingredient that takes them from delicious to delectable. It's also what makes them fun for kids—both to make and to eat!

Kids typically don't care about fancy Riesling reductions or beautifully decorated truffles. They want to be a part of something that tastes good and is *fun*. And isn't licking your fingers clean the most fun? With so much "Careful—that's hot!" or "Watch out—this is sharp!" few things make kids more excited than when you tell them they are actually *allowed* to help in the kitchen. Have your little ones crush the candy for the Sadie (page 101) or stir the pretzels into the peanut butter for the PB&Ps (page 85), and watch their faces light up. And the best part: They can lick their fingers along the way—no raw ingredients that need baking here.

2 teaspoons unsalted butter

3½ cups mini marshmallows

4 cups puffed rice cereal (I like
Rice Krispies)

1 cup gummi bears

2 tablespoons blueberry jam

1 tablespoon water

Use
Kellogg's Rice
Krispies Gluten-
Free cereal to
make this treat
gluten-free.

beary surprise

STICKY ALERT! *The gummi bear glaze on this treat makes them so gluey you can literally throw them against the wall and they will stick. Not that I've tried it…Well, maybe once, but I don't recommend it. It would be such a waste of this chewy little bite!*

◇◇◇◇◇◇◇◇◇◇◇◇◇◇◇◇◇◇ **MAKES ABOUT 20 SERVINGS** ◇◇◇◇◇◇◇◇◇◇◇◇◇◇◇◇◇◇

Line an 8 by 8-inch baking pan with aluminum foil and coat it with nonstick spray. Set aside.

In a large nonstick saucepan, melt the butter over medium heat. Add the marshmallows and stir until melted, 3 to 4 minutes. Remove from the heat and stir in the cereal and ½ cup of the gummi bears.

Using a rubber spatula, spoon the mixture into the prepared pan. Using your hands or a spatula, press the mixture evenly into the bottom.

Place the remaining ½ cup gummi bears, the jam, and the water into a microwave-safe bowl. Microwave on high power in 10-second intervals until completely melted (3 or 4 intervals), stirring after each interval. Pour over the mixture in the pan and spread evenly with a rubber spatula. Allow to firm up at room temperature for 15 minutes.

Cover and refrigerate for 20 minutes (no longer—the treat will get too hard if left in the refrigerator too long) to allow the cereal to soak up the jam–gummi bear juices.

Transfer the sheet to a cutting board. Peel off the foil and cut into two-bite squares with a sharp knife.

our marshmallow

mixture will be very sticky, so you may need to wet your hands or spatula before pressing it down into the pan to help prevent getting stuck. This trick works with most sticky foods, including the Popcorn Balls on page 183—actually, I first learned it while shaping hamburgers!

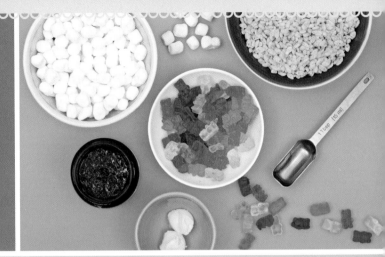

PB&Ps

THESE MAY NOT BECOME *a universal staple like PB&J sandwiches are, but that's only because they're so good that you're going to want to save them for special occasions. Peanut butter and pretzels are a match made in heaven—with their combined tastes and textures leaving a lasting impression in your mouth. Just like those staple sandwiches, they'll wash down perfectly with a glass of milk.*

◇◇◇◇◇◇◇◇◇◇◇◇◇**MAKES ABOUT 20 SERVINGS**◇◇◇◇◇◇◇◇◇◇◇◇◇

Line an 8 by 8-inch baking pan with aluminum foil and coat it with nonstick spray. Set aside.

Add 2 cups of the mini pretzels to a food processor and process until roughly chopped, about 30 seconds. Set aside.

In a small bowl, combine the peanut butter, butter, and brown sugar. Add the chopped pretzels. Stir until the ingredients are distributed evenly. Add the powdered sugar and mix until completely combined; the mixture should thicken quite a bit.

Using a rubber spatula, press the mixture into the bottom of the prepared pan. Refrigerate for 20 minutes.

Melt and temper the chocolate. Pour the chocolate evenly over the mixture, smoothing it with a rubber spatula. Gently tap the pan against a hard surface to even out the chocolate. Place 20 mini pretzels on top, spacing them evenly across the chocolate layer. These will be your guides for cutting your bars.

Transfer to a cutting board. Peel off the foil and cut into two-bite squares with a very sharp knife, with one pretzel sitting in the middle of each bar.

3 cups salted mini pretzels

1 cup salted creamy peanut butter

2 tablespoons unsalted butter, softened

¼ cup tightly packed light brown sugar

10 tablespoons powdered sugar, sifted

1½ cups milk chocolate chopped into quarter-size pieces (or Wilton Candy Melts)

Peanut butter loves to leave a trail wherever it goes. Here is a tip for getting just the right amount—and easily! These PB&Ps call for 1 cup, so you'll need a 2-cup glass measuring cup. Simply fill it with 1 cup of water and add the peanut butter until the water level hits 2 cups. Pour out the water. Ta-da! Perfectly measured peanut butter, minus the stick. This trick will also work for any other hard-to-handle ingredient.

danger squares

2 teaspoons unsalted butter

3½ cups mini marshmallows

4 cups Rice Krispies

1 cup roughly chopped
Butterfinger bars

½ cup peanut butter chips

¼ cup dark chocolate for drizzling

Use Kellogg's Rice Krispies Gluten-Free cereal to make this treat gluten-free.

A FEW YEARS AGO, my niece was nice enough to share her Halloween candy with me. I got to pick three pieces! I chose three mini Butterfingers with a Rice Krispies treat in mind—I had been on an "enhanced" Rice Krispies treat kick. The result was these Danger Squares. After I made them, I simply could not. Stop. Eating. Them. Since then, I've made them for parties and they have a similar effect on everyone. Dangerous, I tell you.

◇◇◇◇◇◇◇◇◇◇◇**MAKES ABOUT 20 SERVINGS**◇◇◇◇◇◇◇◇◇◇◇

Line an 8 by 8-inch baking pan with aluminum foil and grease it with nonstick spray. Set aside.

In a large nonstick saucepan, melt the butter over medium heat. Add the marshmallows and stir until melted, 3 to 4 minutes. Remove from the heat and stir in the cereal, ¾ cup of the Butterfinger pieces, and the peanut butter chips. Using a rubber spatula, spoon the mixture into the prepared pan and press down.

Allow to cool at room temperature for about 10 minutes. In the meantime, prepare the chocolate for drizzling. Drizzle the chocolate onto the mixture and sprinkle with the remaining ¼ cup Butterfinger pieces. Let sit until chocolate has solidified.

Transfer to a cutting board. Peel off the foil and cut into two-bite squares with a sharp knife.

banana crunch bars

- 40 vanilla wafers (I like Nilla Wafers)
- 6 tablespoons unsalted butter, softened
- 2 cups salted or unsalted banana chips
- ¼ cup chocolate-hazelnut spread (I like Nutella)
- 1 cup dark chocolate chopped into quarter-size pieces (or Wilton Candy Melts)
- 1 tablespoon coarse sea salt (optional)

I ABSOLUTELY LOVE BANANA CHIPS. *They are usually made from plantains, which I grew up eating in Miami. There are tons of Cuban recipes that use them, but my favorite by far is tostones. These are basically flattened slices of plantains that are double-fried to become crisp on the outside and soft on the inside. Salt is sprinkled on them before serving. I created the Banana Crunch Bar as an ode to tostones. The flavor is sweet and salty and the texture is crunchy and soft.*

MAKES ABOUT 20 SERVINGS

Line an 8 by 8-inch baking pan with aluminum foil and coat it with nonstick spray. Set aside.

To make the crust, place the vanilla wafers in a food processor and process until fine crumbs form, about 30 seconds. Add the softened butter to the food processor and process for 1 minute. Transfer to a clean bowl.

Press the mixture together with your hands to form a dough and evenly press across the bottom of the prepared pan. Refrigerate for 20 minutes. This will be your crust.

Add banana chips to the food processor and process until pea-size crumbs form, about 30 seconds. Set aside.

Remove the crust from the refrigerator and spread the chocolate-hazelnut spread over the crust evenly using a small rubber spatula. Next, add about half the banana chip crumbs.

CONTINUED

Melt and temper the chocolate (or melt Wilton Candy Melts) and pour over as the next layer. Sprinkle the remaining banana chip crumbs and the salt, if using, over the chocolate. Refrigerate for 45 minutes, or until solid.

Transfer to a cutting board. Peel off the foil and cut into two-bite pieces with a sharp knife.

tostones

2/3 cup vegetable oil

2 large plantains, peeled and cut into 2-inch rounds

Sea salt

Here is a super-easy recipe for those tostones I was talking about. They are a perfect treat anytime—and quick!

◇◇◇◇◇◇◇◇◇◇◇◇◇◇◇**MAKES ABOUT 15**◇◇◇◇◇◇◇◇◇◇◇◇◇◇◇

Heat the oil in a medium skillet over high heat until the temperature reaches 300°F. Add the plantain slices and fry for about 5 minutes, turning them once. Remove from the oil using a slotted spoon and drain on paper towels. Use a plantain press or 2 cutting boards to flatten the plantain slices down to about half their thickness.

Reheat the oil to about 350°F and return the plantains to the pan, frying and turning them until golden brown. Remove from the oil and drain once again on paper towels. Sprinkle with salt.

pecamel fudgey bars

I LOVE THESE BARS BECAUSE they combine two of the most delicious sweets: caramel and fudge. Both are hugely popular but often seem way too complicated to make at home. I hope this recipe will change your mind about that! The fudge and pecan caramel methods here are as simple as can be, without compromising the taste one bit. I love the way they taste together, but you can definitely make them separately if you want to: The fudge is great on its own or with some whipped cream (page 105) on top, and the caramel is perfect for dipping fruit!

◇◇◇◇◇◇◇◇◇◇◇◇◇◇**MAKES ABOUT 20 SERVINGS**◇◇◇◇◇◇◇◇◇◇◇◇◇◇

Line an 8 by 8-inch baking pan with aluminum foil and coat it with nonstick spray. Set aside.

To make the fudge, combine 2½ cups of the chocolate, the condensed milk, and the butter in a large microwave-safe bowl. Microwave on high power in 1-minute increments until melted, stirring after each interval, for 2 to 3 minutes total. Stir until smooth and mixed evenly.

Pour into the prepared pan and smooth into an even layer using a rubber spatula. Place the fudge in the refrigerator for at least 20 minutes while you make your caramel layer.

To make the caramel, stir the sugar, corn syrup, water, and lemon juice together in a 2-cup microwave-safe glass measuring cup or medium glass bowl. Microwave on high power until the mixture begins to take on a slightly golden color, 4 to 7 minutes, depending on your microwave (begin to check on it after about 4 minutes). Let cool for 5 minutes. The caramel will continue to darken.

CONTINUED

FUDGE

3¼ cups dark chocolate chopped into quarter-size pieces (or Wilton Candy Melts) divided

1⅓ cups (one 14-ounce can) sweetened condensed milk

3 tablespoons unsalted butter

PECAN CARAMEL

1 cup granulated sugar

2 tablespoons light corn syrup

2 tablespoons water

⅛ teaspoon lemon juice

½ cup heavy cream

1 tablespoon unsalted butter

1¼ cups coarsely chopped salted pecans

In the meantime, heat the cream in a small saucepan until it comes to a simmer, about 2 minutes. Add the hot cream to your caramel mixture a few tablespoons at a time. It will bubble up intensely, but it shouldn't overflow. Add the butter and stir until melted. Let cool for 5 minutes.

Add the chopped nuts to the caramel and stir briefly. Then pour the caramel-nut mixture over the fudge and smooth into an even layer with your spatula. Place back in the refrigerator for 20 minutes.

Melt and temper the remaining ¾ cup chocolate (or melt Wilton Candy Melts). Spread the chocolate over the fudge, covering all the caramel and nuts in an even layer. Place the fudge in the refrigerator to set for at least 2 hours.

Transfer to a cutting board. Carefully peel off the foil and cut into two-bite squares with a sharp knife. Let sit at room temperature for 10 minutes before serving.

If you'd prefer a more flexible and gooey top layer, skip the tempering and add 1 tablespoon light corn syrup to your remaining chocolate. Microwave in 15-second intervals at medium power until melted. It will adhere nicely to your caramel layer.

marshmallow pretzel bars

THESE BITES WERE BORN FROM *a hitch in my plan to make a plain old batch of Rice Krispies treats. With my marshmallows already melted, I realized I was out of cereal and quickly scoured the pantry for a substitute. I spotted a 12-pack of preportioned mini pretzel pouches, opened them all, chopped them up, and tossed them in with some chocolate and peanut butter. I guarantee this wasn't the intention behind those diet-friendly, 1½-ounce snack bags, but I was in a clear state of emergency.*

◇◇◇◇◇◇◇◇◇◇◇◇◇◇**MAKES ABOUT 20 SERVINGS**◇◇◇◇◇◇◇◇◇◇◇◇◇◇

Line an 8 by 8-inch baking pan with aluminum foil and coat it with nonstick spray. Set aside.

In a large nonstick saucepan, melt the butter over medium heat. Add the marshmallows and stir until melted, 3 to 4 minutes. Remove from the heat and stir in the chocolate chips, peanut butter chips, and pretzel pieces, stirring until the ingredients are evenly distributed.

Using a spatula, press the mixture evenly into the prepared pan. Sprinkle with the salt. Allow to cool for about 20 minutes at room temperature.

Transfer to a cutting board. Peel off the foil and cut into two-bite squares using a sharp knife.

2 teaspoons unsalted butter

3½ cups mini marshmallows

2 tablespoons dark chocolate chips

2 tablespoons peanut butter chips

6 cups roughly chopped or broken salted pretzels

1 teaspoon sea salt

Feel free to substitute the dark chocolate and peanut butter chips with white chocolate and butterscotch chips, or any combination you have handy.

layers o' mint

EVERY YEAR AROUND CHRISTMASTIME *I find myself with an excess of candy canes. Whether they come as part of the gift wrap, are attached to some kind of seasonal company memo, or appear in a child's backpack, they inevitably sneak into our lives. Why not pair up our striped friends with their minty chocolate better halves?*

◇◇◇◇◇◇◇◇◇◇◇◇◇◇**MAKES ABOUT 20 SERVINGS**◇◇◇◇◇◇◇◇◇◇◇◇◇

Line an 8 by 8-inch baking pan with aluminum foil and coat it with nonstick spray. Set aside.

In a large nonstick saucepan, melt the butter over medium heat. Add the marshmallows and stir until melted, 3 to 4 minutes. Remove from the heat and stir in the mint cookies and mint cream–filled candy pieces until evenly distributed. Using a rubber spatula, press the mixture evenly into the prepared pan.

Chop the candy canes and set aside.

Prepare the mint chocolate pieces for drizzling. Drizzle the mint chocolate onto the mixture in the pan and sprinkle it with candy cane pieces.

Allow chocolate to harden before transferring to a cutting board. Peel off the foil and cut into two-bite squares with a very sharp knife.

2 teaspoons unsalted butter

3½ cups mini marshmallows

2 cups roughly chopped mint cookies (I like Thin Mints, but store-brand versions are fine and available year-round)

1 cup roughly chopped chocolate mint cream–filled candies (I like York Peppermint Patties)

1 cup roughly chopped mint chocolate pieces (I like Andes candies)

2 large candy canes, roughly chopped

Chopping candy canes with a knife can be tricky, resulting in pieces flying everywhere. I recommend breaking them up into small pieces with your hands and then using a food processor to do the chopping.

almond butter fudge

1 teaspoon unsalted butter

1 cup sliced almonds

1 cup unsalted creamy
almond butter

¼ cup sweetened condensed milk

1½ tablespoons honey

1 teaspoon ground cinnamon

2 teaspoons sea salt

ALMOND BUTTER IS ONE OF *those foods that is so accessible but for some reason often overlooked. It makes an even better sandwich partner than peanut butter for jelly, an awesome spread on apple slices, and an upgraded topping on brownies. Above all, it makes a great base for a super-delicious no bake treat!*

◇◇◇◇◇◇◇◇◇◇◇◇◇◇◇◇**MAKES ABOUT 20 SERVINGS**◇◇◇◇◇◇◇◇◇◇◇◇◇◇◇◇

Line an 8 by 8-inch baking dish with aluminum foil and coat with nonstick spray. Set aside.

Place the butter in a small sauté pan over low heat. When it is just barely melted, add ½ cup of the sliced almonds and toast until golden brown, about 2 minutes. Remove from the pan and set aside.

Combine the almond butter, condensed milk, honey, cinnamon, 1 teaspoon of the salt, and the remaining untoasted sliced almonds in a large bowl. Using a rubber spatula, stir until evenly distributed. Pour into the prepared pan and smooth into an even layer.

Sprinkle the toasted almonds and the remaining 1 teaspoon salt over the mixture in the pan. Refrigerate for 4 hours or until the fudge is set.

Gently remove the fudge from the pan and place it on a cutting board. Peel off the foil and cut into two-bite pieces.

the sadie

CONTRARY TO POPULAR BELIEF, *brownies need not come out of the oven. The Sadie is a no bake brownie topped with marshmallow fluff and a mishmash of candy. It was inspired by and named for my beautiful brown-eyed niece. She is an absolute sweetie and a candy-monster—just like this treat!*

MAKES ABOUT 20 SERVINGS

Line an 8 by 8-inch baking dish with aluminum foil and coat it with nonstick spray. Set aside.

Place the graham crackers in a food processor and process into a powder consistency. Set aside.

In a medium nonstick saucepan over medium heat, heat the condensed milk with ¼ cup of the chocolate, stirring until completely melted, about 4 minutes, until the mixture just comes to a simmer. Remove from the heat and add the vanilla. Continue stirring for 2 minutes. Add the graham cracker crumbs and stir until evenly distributed. Pour into the prepared pan and refrigerate for 4 hours.

Melt and temper the remaining 1¼ cups chocolate (or melt Wilton Candy Melts) and pour evenly over the top of the mixture in the pan. Refrigerate for 1 hour, or until totally solid.

Using a rubber spatula, spread the marshmallow fluff over the chocolate. Sprinkle the chopped Twix and Reese's Pieces over the marshmallow fluff. Refrigerate for another 30 minutes.

Transfer to a cutting board, peel off the foil, and cut into two-bite squares using a sharp knife.

14 standard chocolate graham cracker sheets

One 14-ounce can sweetened condensed milk

1½ cups milk chocolate cut into quarter-size pieces (or Wilton Candy Melts)

1 teaspoon vanilla extract

¾ cup marshmallow fluff

4 Twix bars (2 packs), roughly chopped

½ cup Reese's Pieces

Feel free to substitute the Twix and Reese's Pieces with your favorite candy!

the sebi

THESE NO BAKE BANANA BLONDIES *are dedicated to my little blond nephew, Sebastian. His mom feeds him fresh fruit slices for breakfast alongside his cereal every morning. He always picks out the bananas first and then asks for more. It's adorable and quite a healthy habit. But needless to say, he loves these blondies even more!*

◇◇◇◇◇◇◇◇◇◇◇◇◇◇◇◇**MAKES ABOUT 20 SERVINGS**◇◇◇◇◇◇◇◇◇◇◇◇◇◇◇

Line an 8 by 8-inch baking dish with aluminum foil and coat it with nonstick spray. Set aside.

Place the vanilla wafers in a food processor and process until they reach a powder consistency. Set aside.

Cut 1 banana into small pieces and set aside.

In a medium nonstick saucepan over medium heat, heat the condensed milk along with ¼ cup of the white chocolate, stirring until completely blended. Once the chocolate is melted, about 4 minutes, and is at a slow boil, remove from the heat and add the vanilla. Continue stirring for 2 minutes. Add the vanilla wafer crumbs and banana pieces and stir until evenly distributed. Pour into the prepared pan and refrigerate for 2 hours.

Melt and temper the remaining 1¼ cups white chocolate (or melt Wilton Candy melts) and pour it evenly over the top of the no bake blondie mix. Refrigerate for 1 hour, or until totally solid.

Transfer to a cutting board. Peel off the foil and cut into two-bite squares using a sharp knife.

Cut the second banana into ½-inch slices. Top each square with a dollop of whipped cream and a slice of banana.

80 vanilla wafers (I like Nilla Wafers)

2 bananas

1 cup sweetened condensed milk

1½ cups white chocolate chopped into quarter-size pieces (or Wilton Candy Melts)

1 teaspoon vanilla extract

1 cup homemade whipped cream (recipe follows), or store-bought

quick whipped cream

1 cup heavy cream

1 tablespoon granulated sugar

½ teaspoon vanilla extract

Here is a quick, useful, and delicious whipped cream recipe. It is referenced in several recipes throughout the book.

ABOUT 2 CUPS

Combine the cream, sugar, and vanilla in a large bowl and mix with an electric mixer (or in a food processor) at medium speed until soft peaks form, 2 to 3 minutes.

Yes, you can use a food processor to whip your cream! Just pour the ingredients in and process for 1 to 2 minutes, until the correct consistency is reached—soft peaks. Perfect fluffy goodness.

Mini Pies
AND
Cakes

Achapter on pies and cakes might seem a bit odd in a no bake book. After all, the defining characteristic of both is that they are *baked* goods! But even though some of my favorite desserts are non-oven treats, I am still human. A human who loves cakes and pies, just like the rest of the world.

One of my favorite parts of my wedding planning was the cake tasting. I remember asking the bakery if my husband and I could try just one more bite to double-check that it was the right one. The cake also made a stunning addition to the reception—cutting into the beautiful layers of buttercream with my new husband to reveal a perfectly light and moist cake inside. Few memories can top that.

Like cakes, pies are usually reserved for special occasions. In fact, my friend Christina opted for no cake, just mini pies, at her North Carolina barn wedding. While we went the more traditional route, I certainly understood her choice. I must have heard more than fifteen guests comment on how cute and delicious they were. Pies are an American staple, and their flaky crusts and creamy, fruity fillings bring so much joy to a celebration.

While these treats are both special enough to be showcased on your special day, they've been known to make their way into *any* fun day. They can be found in grade-school classrooms or offices for no reason at all; they even pop up on a blanketed picnic in Central Park just because it's a sunny day. Oven or no oven, there was definitely no way I was going to omit yummy cakes and cutie pies from this book. The refrigerator—almost the opposite of the oven—will be our friend here. And I promise, these recipes are a piece of cake, or at least as easy as pie.

to create

vertical hearts, drizzle melted Wilton Candy Melts into shapes on a piece of wax paper and allow to harden. Carefully remove them from the wax paper and insert them into your cakes.

pink velvet cheesecake

REAL LOVE DOESN'T COME EASY. *It takes patience and hard work to show some-one you love them. Why not make things a little easier for yourself? Perfect for Valentine's Day but welcomed on any occasion, Pink Velvet Cheesecake is the tastiest way to show love without even breaking a sweat. It's gooey in the center and sweet all around—fun and a little bit messy, just like love.*

◇◇◇◇◇◇◇◇◇◇◇◇◇◇◇◇◇►**MAKES 24 TREATS**◄◇◇◇◇◇◇◇◇◇◇◇◇◇◇◇◇◇

Line a mini muffin tin with foil or paper liners and set aside.

To make the crust, in a food processor, process the graham crackers until fine crumbs form, about 30 seconds. Add the softened butter and process until thickened. Transfer to a clean bowl.

Using a rounded teaspoon or a cookie scoop, spoon the mixture into the prepared cups. Press the mixture against the bottom and sides of each cup to form a shell. Place the tin in the freezer for 30 minutes.

To make the filling, in a deep bowl, combine the gelatin and water. Let sit for 5 minutes.

Meanwhile, combine the cream, cream cheese, sweetened condensed milk, red food coloring, and 4½ tablespoons of the white chocolate chips in the food processor and process until combined. Your mixture should be hot pink.

After 5 minutes have passed, microwave the gelatin water for 10 seconds—no longer. Add the warmed gelatin water to the food processor and blend again for a few seconds to combine. Using a rounded tea-spoon or cookie scoop, spoon the mixture into the pie shells. Refrigerate for at least 5 hours or overnight.

Prepare the remaining white chocolate chips for drizzling. Drizzle each cake as you wish.

CRUST

8 standard graham cracker sheets

3 tablespoons unsalted butter, softened

FILLING

1⅛ teaspoons unflavored gelatin (found in the baking section of your grocery store; I like Knox brand)

4½ tablespoons water, at room temperature

¾ cup heavy cream

6 ounces cream cheese, softened (I recommend using light or ⅓ fat)

3 ounces sweetened condensed milk

1½ teaspoons red food coloring

¾ cup white chocolate chips

Note that you do not need to stir the gelatin into the water. Simply let the gelatin powder sit on top of the liquid and it will become gelatinous after a few minutes.

applesauce cake

APPLE DESSERTS COME IN ALL *shapes, sizes, and flavors. Apple popovers, apple strudels, apple tarts, apple pies—you name it. But one of my favorite apple treats is plain ol' applesauce. Its smooth texture and natural sweetness make it the perfect guilt-free snack. In this soft cake, I've partnered applesauce with crumbly layers to enhance its subtle flavor and maintain its creamy texture. How do you like them apples?*

◇◇◇◇◇◇◇◇◇◇◇◇◇◇◇MAKES ABOUT 20 SERVINGS◇◇◇◇◇◇◇◇◇◇◇◇◇◇◇

Melt the butter in a small bowl in the microwave. Stir the cinnamon into the hot melted butter. Mix thoroughly with the gingersnap crumbs.

Press half the crumb mixture into the bottom of the prepared pan, using a spatula to pack it down firmly.

In a medium mixing bowl, combine the applesauce and ¾ teaspoon of the lemon juice. Spread ¾ cup of the mixture over the bottom crumb layer in the pan. Top with the remaining crumbs and spread the rest of the applesauce-lemon juice mixture on top. Place the pan in the freezer while preparing the apples and whipped cream.

Thinly slice the apple (a mandoline slicer or your food processor's slicing blade makes quick work of this) and place in a bowl with the remaining lemon juice to prevent browning. Cover the bowl loosely, place in the microwave, and poach the apple slices until just tender, about 45 seconds. Drain and dispose of the lemon juice. Remove the pan from the freezer. Top the cake with whipped cream and garnish with apple slices. Refrigerate for 5 hours or overnight. Cut into mini slices.

3 tablespoons unsalted butter

1 teaspoon ground cinnamon

1½ cups finely crushed crisp gingersnap cookies (6 ounces)

1½ cups unsweetened applesauce

Juice of 1 lemon

½ Granny Smith apple, peeled and thinly sliced

1 cup homemade whipped cream (page 105), or store-bought

caramel cream

¼ cup granulated sugar

1 tablespoon water, at room temperature

Pinch of salt

1 cup heavy cream

If you'd like a richer and sweeter cake, skip the regular whipped cream and go for this delicious caramel cream instead.

MAKES ABOUT 2 CUPS

In a large nonstick saucepan over medium heat, heat the sugar, water, and salt, stirring until the sugar is dissolved. Continue cooking, without stirring, until the sugar turns golden.

Remove the pan from the heat and slowly pour in ½ cup of the cream. Return the pan to medium heat and stir with a wooden spoon until combined. Remove from the heat and stir in the remaining ½ cup cream until the mixture is smooth.

Strain the caramel cream into a deep medium bowl. Cover and refrigerate until chilled, at least 2 hours or overnight.

Whip the cream with an electric mixer (or use a food processor; see page 105) until stiff peaks form, 2 to 3 minutes.

coconilla pie

LIVING IN BROOKLYN IS GREAT, *but sometimes a Caribbean getaway is just what the doctor ordered. After about a year in New York, we vacationed underneath the coconut trees of Aruba and loved every minute of it. Every day a tanned local woman would sell coconut pies and coconut milk on the beach. I was almost jealous of her—my husband gave her treats a lot of attention. Well, if you can't beat them, join them, right? I remixed this pie as a way to bring us back to that vacation whenever we need a break from the daily grind— and to subtly remind my husband that my treats are the greatest!*

 **MAKES 24 TREATS**

Line a mini muffin tin with foil or paper liners and set aside.

To make the crust, place the vanilla wafers in a food processor and process until fine crumbs form, about 60 seconds. Add the softened butter and cream cheese and mix until thickened. Transfer to a bowl.

Using a rounded teaspoon or a cookie scoop, spoon the mixture into the prepared tin. Press the mixture against the bottom and sides of the cups to form a pie shell. Place in the freezer for 30 minutes.

In the meantime, to make the pie filling, combine the sugar, cornstarch, and salt in a medium nonstick saucepan over medium heat. Gradually stir in the milk and keep stirring until thickened and bubbly, about 2 minutes. Reduce the heat and stir for another 2 minutes. Remove from the heat.

Lightly beat the egg yolks in a small bowl. Stir in 3 tablespoons of the warm milk mixture, and then pour the mixture back into the saucepan. Over medium heat, stir constantly and bring to a gentle boil, about 1 minute. Remove from the heat and continue stirring for 2 to 3 minutes. Add the butter and vanilla. Continue stirring until completely combined and smooth.

CONTINUED

CRUST
35 vanilla wafers (I like Nilla Wafers)

3 tablespoons unsalted butter, softened

3 tablespoons cream cheese, softened (I recommend using light or 1/3 fat)

FILLING
1/4 cup granulated sugar

2 tablespoons cornstarch

1/4 teaspoon salt

2 cups skim milk

2 egg yolks

2 1/2 teaspoons unsalted butter

1 teaspoon vanilla extract

1 cup coconut flakes

Transfer the wet mixture from the pan to a clean bowl and stir in ¾ cup of the coconut flakes. Press a piece of wax paper (or parchment lightly coated with nonstick spray) onto the pudding surface to prevent it from forming a skin as it cools. Allow to cool for 30 minutes at room temperature.

Using a rounded tablespoon or cookie scoop, spoon the pudding into the pie shells. Refrigerate for 1 hour or until set. Sprinkle the pies with the remaining ¼ cup coconut flakes.

When forming pie shells, it is best to begin with the cups in the center of your muffin tin so you can use the surrounding empty cups as a grip while you shape the mini crusts.

for a savory treat,

spoon a tiny bit of goat cheese into the piecrusts before adding the fig filling. These make for an impressive two-bite hors d'oeuvre.

mini fig pies

EVERY SUMMER OUR ITALIAN LANDLADY, Rose, leaves fresh fruits and vegetables from her garden on our staircase. I get so excited for the tomatoes, zucchini, peppers—you name it. The only one I wouldn't get so excited about is the figs. Their look and texture would always turn me off, with their leathery skin and very mushy consistency. Well, one day the fig basket from Rose was extra-big and I thought, I've got to do something with these. I called my mom and asked her if she had any ideas, and she said I should try to make them into a jam, similar to a Fig Newton filling. I took my first stab at fig jam and started to gain an appreciation for the fruit. Eventually I added the jam to one of my favorite piecrusts, and the result was simply delicious. What I once thought was an ugly fruit turned into a cute-as-can-be pie.

◇◇◇◇◇◇◇◇◇◇◇◇◇◇◇◇◇◇**MAKES 24 TREATS**◇◇◇◇◇◇◇◇◇◇◇◇◇◇◇◇◇◇

Line a mini muffin tin with foil or paper liners and set aside.

To make the crust, combine the walnuts and graham crackers in a food processor and process until fine crumbs form, about 1 minute. Add the coconut oil and process until a dough begins to form, about 30 seconds.

Using a rounded teaspoon or a cookie scoop, spoon the mixture into the prepared tin. Press the mixture against the bottom and sides of the cups to form pie shells. Place in the freezer for 1 hour.

To make the filling, place the figs, lemon juice, and brown sugar in a food processor and process for about 30 seconds, until a jam begins to form. Transfer to a bowl, cover with plastic wrap, and refrigerate for about 1 hour.

Using a rounded tablespoon or a cookie scoop, spoon the fig jam into the pie shells. Refrigerate for 2 hours.

CRUST

½ cup chopped walnuts

6 standard graham cracker sheets

3 tablespoons coconut oil
(I recommend using virgin oil)

FILLING

30 dried figs (6 ounces) (I like Mission brand)

2 tablespoons fresh lemon juice

¼ cup firmly packed light brown sugar

Even though Rose may not be delivering them to your doorstep, use fresh figs if you can find them in the summer! They are in peak season in August and September. If using fresh figs, make sure you add another couple of teaspoons of brown sugar, or to taste, as they are less sweet than the dried ones.

PB & banilla icebox cake

40 vanilla wafers (I like Nilla Wafers)

1 cup heavy cream

1 tablespoon granulated sugar

½ teaspoon banana extract

¼ cup salted creamy organic peanut butter

2 tablespoons peanut butter chips

2 large bananas

1 teaspoon ground cinnamon (optional)

Using organic peanut butter is important for this recipe, specifically because it's way soupier than conventional creamy peanut butter. You'll need it to be thin in order to fold it into the whipped cream. A heavy variety would deflate your cream.

I MADE PEANUT BUTTER WHIPPED CREAM *just to have in the house (normal, right?) and found so many uses for it. I added it to frozen yogurt one night and spread it onto banana slices the next. By the time I found myself sneaking into the refrigerator and eating it by the spoonful, I knew I had to use up the rest of it in a hurry. And so this icebox cake was born. It was by far the whipped cream's best use. Why this ingredient is not in more desserts, I do not know. Peanut butter has such a bold flavor; adding it to a relatively flavorless (but texture-rich) whipped cream makes it the best complement. What used to be my sneaky spoonful has become a favorite two-bite delight.*

◇◇◇◇◇◇◇◇◇◇◇**MAKES ABOUT 20 SERVINGS**◇◇◇◇◇◇◇◇◇◇◇◇◇◇◇

Line an 8 by 8-inch baking pan with aluminum foil. Set aside.

Create a vanilla wafer layer along the bottom of the pan with about 20 wafers. You may need to break some up to get them to fit just right.

In a large bowl, beat the cream with the sugar and banana extract using an electric mixer on high speed until soft peaks form, 2 to 3 minutes (or use a food processor; see page 105). Transfer the mixture to a clean bowl and gently fold in the peanut butter and peanut butter chips. Be careful not to deflate your cream.

Spread about half of the peanut butter–banana whipped cream over the wafer layer in the pan using a small rubber spatula.

Very thinly slice 1 banana and layer the slices on top of the cream. Repeat the layering process with the remaining wafers and cream. Cover with plastic wrap and refrigerate overnight.

CONTINUED

Very thinly slice the second banana and spread the slices over the top. Sprinkle with cinnamon, if using. Cut into 1-inch squares.

For an extra-yummy and classy-looking cake, caramelize your top layer of banana. To do this, heat 1 teaspoon butter and 1 teaspoon honey in a medium sauté pan over medium heat until barely melted. Add ½-inch-thick banana slices and cook until golden brown, turning once. Drain on paper towels before adding them as the top layer of your cake.

apple jack pie

WHEN MY NIECE WAS *about two years old and just beginning to speak, I was enamored with how cute everything she said sounded. So much so that after greeting her with a big hug, I would say one of the "cute words" just so she would repeat it after me. Up there on the top of the list right next to "butterfly" was "apple pie." To this day, I recall this game with her, and she'll still say it in what she now refers to as a baby voice: "ap-pull pieeeee." This memory inspired me to put a twist on the classic apple pie by adding some of our favorite child-hood treats: Apple Jacks! The tartness from the apples and the tanginess from the yogurt in a filling sitting on a sweet and salty crust makes this mini pie just a little more fun. Just like saying "ap-pull pieeeee!"*

◇◇◇◇◇◇◇◇◇◇◇◇◇◇**MAKES 24 TREATS**◇◇◇◇◇◇◇◇◇◇◇◇◇◇

Line a mini muffin tin with paper liners or foil liners. Set aside.

To make the crust, place the cookies, cereal, and salt in a food processor and process until fine crumbs form, about 1 minute. Add the softened butter and process until the mixture begins to thicken, about 30 seconds. Transfer to a clean bowl.

Using a rounded tablespoon or cookie scoop, spoon the mixture into the prepared tin. Press the mixture against the bottom and sides of the cups to form pie shells. Place in the freezer for 30 minutes.

Meanwhile, in a small saucepan over medium heat, cook the chopped apple, butter, brown sugar, cinnamon, and nutmeg, stirring occasionally, until the apple is tender, 8 to 10 minutes. Remove from the heat and stir in the vanilla. Transfer to a clean bowl, cover with plastic wrap, and refrigerate for about 30 minutes.

Sprinkle the gelatin over the apple juice in a small bowl and allow to soften for 5 minutes.

CONTINUED

CRUST

22 shortbread cookies (the small square kind work well—I like Lorna Doone)

½ cup Apple Jacks (store brand also works fine), plus more for garnish

¼ teaspoon salt

4 tablespoons (½ stick) unsalted butter, softened

FILLING

1 cup peeled and coarsely chopped Granny Smith apple (about 1 medium apple)

2 tablespoons unsalted butter

2 tablespoons firmly packed light brown sugar

½ teaspoon ground cinnamon

Pinch of ground nutmeg

¼ teaspoon vanilla extract

1 teaspoon unflavored gelatin (found in the baking section of your grocery store; I like Knox brand)

3 tablespoons apple juice

½ cup sweetened condensed milk

¼ cup plain lowfat or nonfat Greek yogurt (do not substitute another type of yogurt—Greek yogurt has the perfect tart flavor)

though any apple

variety could work in this recipe, Granny Smith apples are recommended—they are very tart, which makes them perfect for desserts.

Add the condensed milk and yogurt to the food processor and process until combined. Microwave the gelatin-juice mixture until the gelatin is dissolved, 15 to 20 seconds. With the processor running, pour the gelatin-juice mixture into the machine and process until smooth.

Scrape the mixture into the bowl containing the cooled apples and fold in with a spatula until well combined. Spoon the mixture into the prepared shells and refrigerate for 2 hours. Garnish with Apple Jacks before serving.

cornflake fudge pie

YEARS AGO I STUMBLED UPON *this pie's baked counterpart: the brownie pie, which contains a brownie baked inside a piecrust. While it was obviously delicious, the brownie texture was too similar to the crust texture. I do love the idea of giving a normally naked sweet its own little shell, so I invented a no bake cousin. The brownie might not have been quite right for the job, but fudge definitely does the trick. Its velvety texture is the perfect complement to a crumbly crust.*

◇◇◇◇◇◇◇◇◇◇◇◇◇◇◇◇◇◇◇**MAKES 24 TREATS**◇◇◇◇◇◇◇◇◇◇◇◇◇◇◇◇◇

Line a mini muffin tin with aluminum foil or paper liners and set aside.

To form the crust, place 1 cup of the cornflakes in a food processer and process until fine crumbs form, about 30 seconds. Add 4 tablespoons of the butter and the sugar and process until the mixture begins to thicken. Transfer to a clean bowl.

Using a rounded tablespoon or cookie scoop, spoon the mixture into the prepared tin. Press the mixture against the bottom and sides of the cups to form pie shells. Place in the freezer for 30 minutes.

In the meantime, to make the filling, in a large microwave-safe bowl, combine the chocolate, the remaining 1 tablespoon butter, and the condensed milk. Stir well and microwave for 2 minutes in 15-second intervals at medium power, stirring after each interval, until the chocolate and butter are melted. Mix until the ingredients are completely blended. Stir in the pecans and the remaining 1½ cups cornflakes. Cool at room temperature for 20 minutes.

Spoon the mixture into the prepared shells and refrigerate for at least 5 hours or overnight.

2½ cups cornflakes (store brand is fine)

5 tablespoons unsalted butter, softened

2 teaspoons granulated sugar

1 cup dark chocolate chopped into quarter-size pieces (or Wilton Candy Melts)

½ cup sweetened condensed milk

¼ cup chopped roasted pecans

key lime pie

GROWING UP IN MIAMI MEANT *a lot of vacationing in the Florida Keys—which meant my fair share of Key lime pie. One of the first times my then boyfriend (now husband) came to visit my family, we managed to eat Key lime pie three times in a mere forty-eight hours. At every restaurant we visited during that trip, someone at the table would declare that "this place has the best key lime pie," and another pie would bite the dust. What can I say? Floridians—myself included—know their Key limes.*

◇◇◇◇◇◇◇◇◇◇◇◇◇◇◇◇◇◇◇**MAKES 24 TREATS**◇◇◇◇◇◇◇◇◇◇◇◇◇◇◇◇◇◇◇

Line a mini muffin tin with foil or paper liners and set aside.

To make the crust, combine the pretzels and sugar in a food processor and process until medium crumbs form (do not overprocess into a powder), about 30 seconds. Add the softened butter and process until the mixture begins to thicken. Transfer to a clean bowl.

Using a rounded tablespoon or cookie scoop, spoon the mixture into the prepared tin. Press the mixture against the bottom and sides of the cups to form pie shells. Place in the freezer for 30 minutes.

To make the filling, in a large bowl, combine the cream cheese, Key lime juice, condensed milk, lime zest, and vanilla. Mix well with an electric mixer (you can also use a food processor) for about 4 minutes, until completely combined.

Spoon the mixture into the prepared shells. Tap the pie pan against a hard surface to even out the filling. Refrigerate for 1 hour. Garnish with the whipped cream and the lime zest.

> Peak season for Key limes is June to August. If you can't find Key limes you can substitute regular Persian limes, though the result will be a little different. Key limes are more tart and bitter than regular limes, giving Key lime pie that extra-sour punch it's known for.

CRUST

2 cups (4 ounces) salted pretzel sticks

½ cup granulated sugar

½ cup (1 stick) unsalted butter, softened

FILLING

3 tablespoons cream cheese, softened (I recommend using light or ⅓ fat)

¼ cup fresh Key lime juice

½ cup sweetened condensed milk

½ teaspoon Key lime zest, plus extra for garnish

¼ teaspoon vanilla extract

½ cup homemade whipped cream (page 105), or store-bought

strawberry nutella icebox cake

THE FIRST TIME I MADE *this cake, my friend immediately snapped a picture and uploaded it to her Facebook page. Caption: Yum. She got more "likes" on that photo than she's ever gotten before! The first comment on the post was "Get in ma belly!" Simply put, this is an impressive cake. The layers make it look really fancy, and strawberry and chocolate make an irresistible combination. The best part? It's insanely easy to make.*

MAKES ABOUT 20 SERVINGS

Line an 8 by 8-inch baking pan with aluminum foil and set aside.

Combine the cream, sugar, cinnamon, and vanilla in a large bowl and mix with an electric mixer (or a food processor; see page 105) until soft peaks form, 3 to 4 minutes. Transfer to a clean bowl and gently fold in the chocolate-hazelnut spread. Be careful not to mix too aggressively or your cream will deflate.

Line the prepared pan with graham crackers. You may have to break a few pieces to get them to fit just right. Top with a thick layer of chocolate-hazelnut whipped cream. Next, place 1 cup sliced strawberries over the cream evenly—they should sink in a bit. Repeat the layering process twice, ending with cream. Your cake will have 3 layers of graham crackers, 3 layers of cream, and 2 layers of strawberries. Cover and refrigerate for at least 6 hours or overnight.

Garnish with the remaining sliced strawberries and cut into 1-inch slices.

3 cups heavy cream

2 tablespoons granulated sugar

½ teaspoon ground cinnamon

2 teaspoons vanilla extract

½ cup chocolate-hazelnut spread (I like Nutella)

15 standard cinnamon graham cracker sheets

2½ cups thinly sliced strawberries

it is important

that you do not replace the whole milk in this recipe. Using lowfat or skim milk in panna cotta will cause it to fall apart easily. Panna cotta is a very delicate treat, especially when made in mini form.

grape panna cotta pies

PANNA COTTA IS ITALIAN for "cooked cream." Some versions of this dessert are just that—no toppings, no flavors, nothing. But luckily it can be served several ways. Right after I got engaged, my husband took me on a surprise trip to Italy (marry an amazing guy: check). With panna cotta listed as dolce at virtually every ristorante, I took this as an opportunity to do some "research" on which flavors best complemented the cream, from caramel to ricotta to chocolate to fruit. I decided my favorite style was that which stayed closest to the original, simple form and didn't overpower the cream. I returned to Brooklyn a "seasoned tester" and created this recipe—just a little grape juice, lemon, and sugar go a long way.

MAKES 24 TREATS

½ cup whole milk

1½ teaspoons unflavored gelatin (found in the baking section of your grocery store; I like Knox brand)

2 tablespoons granulated sugar

Pinch of salt

1½ cups heavy cream

¼ cup white grape juice

1 teaspoon vanilla extract

½ teaspoon fresh lemon juice

Sliced grapes for garnish

Grease a mini muffin tin with nonstick spray and set aside.

Pour the milk into a small bowl and evenly sprinkle the gelatin over it. Let stand for 5 minutes.

Pour the milk-gelatin mixture into a small heavy nonstick saucepan and stir over medium heat just until the gelatin is no longer visible but the mixture does not boil, about 2 minutes. Remove from the heat and add the sugar and salt to the pan, stirring until dissolved. Return the pan to medium heat and, stirring constantly, slowly add the cream. Continue to cook, stirring, for another 2½ minutes, until completely combined.

Remove from the heat and stir in the grape juice, vanilla, and lemon juice.

Pour the mixture into mini muffin tin cups and refrigerate until set, at least 6 hours or overnight.

Press lightly with your fingertips on the outer edges of the panna cotta pies to loosen from the tin. Garnish with grape slices.

retro cake

30 chocolate wafer cookies (I like Nabisco)

3 tablespoons cold water

1 packet (1 tablespoon) unflavored gelatin (found in the baking section of your grocery store; I like Knox brand)

¾ cup frozen raspberries

¾ cup frozen blueberries

¾ cup granulated sugar

2 cups cold heavy cream

1 teaspoon vanilla extract

When layering the cookies at the bottom of the pan, don't worry if they don't fit perfectly. This part of the process does not have to be flawless; a few broken pieces here or there won't affect the final product.

THIS RECIPE IS AN OLDIE *but a goodie. In the 1920s everybody who was anybody was making icebox cakes in the freezer using Nabisco wafer cookies. With air conditioners few and far between, they were a warm-weather party staple. In this recipe, by inserting the wafers into the middle of the cake and mixing fruit to make it purple, I've enhanced its retro status. The bright color, funky pattern, and cold temperature prove that this one is still the "it" cake for a summertime party.*

MAKES ABOUT 20 SERVINGS

Line an 8 by 8-inch pan with aluminum foil and set aside.

Line the bottom of the pan with cookies (about 20). You may need to break some up to get them to fit just right.

Pour the cold water into a small bowl and sprinkle the gelatin over the water; let sit for 2 minutes.

Combine the raspberries, blueberries, and sugar in a medium heavy saucepan and cook over medium-low heat, stirring a few times, until the sugar dissolves and the mixture becomes warm to the touch. Stir in the gelatin mixture. Remove from the heat and let cool to room temperature, stirring occasionally. Set aside.

Combine the heavy cream and vanilla in a large bowl and mix using an electric mixer (or use a food processor; see page 105) until stiff peaks form, 3 to 4 minutes. Gently fold in the cooled raspberry mixture, taking care not to deflate the cream.

Pour about half the mixture into the prepared pan and smooth it with a rubber spatula. Insert the remaining wafers into the mousse vertically (this will make your cross section look cool when you slice it later). Spread the remaining mousse over the wafers and smooth with the spatula. Cover with plastic wrap and freeze overnight.

CONTINUED

Transfer the cake to a cutting board. Peel away the plastic wrap and slice into 1-inch squares.

The peak season for raspberries and blueberries is June through August. If they are in season, feel free to use fresh instead of frozen!

Cold Cravings
AND
Pudding

There comes a time around the end of June when my husband and I crave ice cream. Every. Single. Day. It lasts all the way through the end of the summer.

It begins fairly innocently with a "Hey, babe, want to go grab gelato?" The answer is always yes, of course, and so we'll walk the fifty steps over to our local Italian pastry shop that serves *the* most wonderful gelato. I usually order stracciatella and he goes for dulce de leche.

By August, initiating the ritual requires little more than eye contact. After we finish dinner, we glance at each other with "the look." It precedes a few "No, no, we shouldn't" exchanges, but most of the time we go anyway. Both inspired by the shop's ability to keep us coming back for more and slightly embarrassed by the need to create an ice cream budget, I decided to take measures into my own hands. I began jotting down recipe ideas for cold, refreshing desserts and adding them to my no bake repertoire.

If you want something cold on hot days (and I know we aren't alone here), this chapter is for you. Many people make dessert all the time but rule out the possibility of making frozen treats—for some reason they seem inaccessible. Perhaps because most chilled recipes require an ice cream machine, ice pop molds, or other fancy equipment. This gear is great—in fact, I recommend owning it! But you certainly do not *need* any of it to make yourself some cold treats.

This chapter offers a bunch of easy-to-make treats that will give you that extra chill. They're all meant to be served cold—and even better, to prevent the inevitable frozen yogurt/ice cream/smoothie/gelato run.

tira, sue me

TIRAMISU IN ITALIAN TRANSLATES TO *"pick-me-up." This is in reference to the espresso used in most traditional recipes for the dessert. Staying true to the "pick-me-up" credo, I've cut the proportions to make this one mini but upped the espresso. While most desserts can leave you feeling a bit sluggish, this one will both satisfy your sweet tooth and make you more productive! I know it may seem like a crime to fiddle with a treat as perfect as tiramisu, but I promise this cup of goodness is worth the tampering. So go ahead and try out this tiramisu remix treat—you won't get sued!*

◇◇◇◇◇◇◇◇◇◇◇◇◇◇◇◇MAKES 15 1½-OUNCE SERVINGS◇◇◇◇◇◇◇◇◇◇◇◇◇◇◇

Place the ladyfingers in a food processor and process until fine crumbs form, about 1 minute. Transfer to a bowl and set aside.

Whisk the sugar, vanilla, mascarpone, and espresso together in a medium bowl until the ingredients are evenly distributed.

Spoon just under a tablespoon of ladyfinger crumbs into the bottom of a shot glass or other mini serving vessel. Then spoon in a little less than 1 tablespoon of the mascarpone mixture as the next layer. Repeat one more time.

Refrigerate for at least 3 hours or overnight. Sprinkle with the cocoa powder and cinnamon before serving.

24 ladyfinger cookies (I like Gilda brand)

½ cup granulated sugar

2 teaspoons vanilla extract

1 cup mascarpone cheese

¼ cup brewed espresso

2 tablespoons cocoa powder

4 teaspoons ground cinnamon

best banana
ice cream

8 large ripe bananas, frozen

1 cup chopped walnuts

½ cup creamy salted
peanut butter

½ cup firmly packed brown sugar

For an *extra*-low-calorie
version, skip the brown
sugar entirely and cut
the peanut butter in half.
While the treat won't taste
as decadent, the banana's
natural sweetness will
still be present, and this
cold treat is sure to still
be yummy.

"TOO GOOD TO BE TRUE" *is a common phrase that is often proven true, sadly. Sixty percent off these fabulous heels! Not really—you must spend a minimum of $250 and open a store credit card account. Just 70 calories per container of yogurt! Nope—70 calories per serving, and there are three servings in this tiny cup! However, this ice cream is one treat that defies the odds and the old adage. If you've ever made ice cream at home, you know how difficult it can be. You have to use specialized equipment, often rock salt, and of course milk. Well, all this ice cream needs is a blender, frozen bananas, some walnuts, peanut butter, and a bit of brown sugar to sweeten the deal. How does the taste compare to the original? It's even* better! *And with a fraction of the calories and fat, it's guilt-free to boot!*

◇◇◇◇◇◇◇◇◇◇**MAKES ABOUT 20 1½-OUNCE SERVINGS**◇◇◇◇◇◇◇◇◇◇

Allow your frozen bananas to thaw for 5 minutes. Cut the bananas down the middle lengthwise and peel each half.

Combine the frozen bananas, chopped walnuts, peanut butter, and brown sugar in a food processor and process until ice cream forms, 2 to 3 minutes.

Scoop into mini bowls or the mini serving vessels of your choice.

One 20-ounce can crushed
pineapple, unsweetened

1 small box (¾ ounce) instant
pistachio pudding mix (I like
Jell-O brand)

1 cup homemade whipped cream
(page 105), or store-bought

½ cup mini marshmallows

3 cups shelled pistachios, finely
chopped

pistachio party

WHEN I FIRST SHARED THE NEWS *of this book with my girlfriends, quite a few recipe suggestions rolled in. A bunch of recipes with the no bake theme had been handed down from generations past. This suggestion, an old school pudding salad classic, was one of my favorites. My friend Anna's family originally named it Shut the Gate Salad because it is so good that when you know it's going to be served you run to "shut the gate" so no one else can come in and you don't have to share! By breaking up the pudding with layers of salty pistachio pieces and portioning it into mini servings, I've kept it just as tasty but now it's inherently sharable. You can leave the gate open and invite friends to this Pistachio Party.*

◇◇◇◇◇◇◇◇◇◇MAKES ABOUT 30 1½-OUNCE SERVINGS◇◇◇◇◇◇◇◇◇◇

In a large bowl, combine the pineapple and the pudding mix, stirring together until well blended. Fold in the whipped cream and mini marshmallows. Cover and refrigerate for 2 hours or until set.

Spoon just under a tablespoon of the mixture into shot glasses or mini serving vessels of your choice. Add just under a tablespoon of chopped pistachios as the next layer. Repeat one more time.

star bursts

IF YOU ARE A FAN *of tart flavors, this treat is for you. The delicate sourness of the Greek yogurt is accentuated by the lemon and orange juice tang. Pop in one of the most beloved tart candies, Starbursts, and you've got yourself a lip-smacking pop. While these are in the freezer, the candies will release some of their color into the pops, resulting in a tie-dye effect. The finished product reminds me of fireworks, making this one perfect for the Fourth of July.*

◇◇◇◇◇◇◇◇◇◇◇◇◇◇◇**MAKES ABOUT 30 TREATS**◇◇◇◇◇◇◇◇◇◇◇◇◇◇◇

2 cups Greek yogurt

3 tablespoons fresh lemon juice

½ cup fresh orange juice

15 ice pop sticks, cut in half

30 Starburst candies

Combine the yogurt, lemon juice, and orange juice in a large bowl. Using a rubber spatula, stir until evenly blended.

Spoon the yogurt mixture into ice cube trays, filling each opening about three-quarters full. Tap the tray against a hard surface to even out the mixture.

Stick the blunt side of an ice pop stick into a Starburst and place one in each ice cube slot. Tap the tray against a hard surface again to even it out.

Freeze for 4 hours, or until solid. Carefully flex the tray to release the pops.

If you use nonfat yogurt for this recipe, its water content will crystallize while the pops are freezing, resulting in a grainier texture. If you'd prefer your treats smoother, opt for 2% or full fat. It's totally up to you.

baby ice cream sandwiches

2 large egg yolks

½ cup granulated sugar

1 teaspoon vanilla extract

½ teaspoon salt

6 ounces evaporated milk

¾ cup heavy cream

40 mini chocolate chip cookies
(I like Famous Amos)

MY NAME IS CRISTINA, *and I am addicted to Chipwiches. I blame this weakness on Richard LaMotta. He, the inventor of the Chipwich, began a guerrilla marketing campaign in 1981 in which he trained and hired a hundred street cart vendors to sell the Chipwich on the streets of New York City. Since then the Chipwich has infiltrated the market, sneaking its way into corner stores, vending machines, camps, and pool snack bars everywhere. They have been impossible to avoid for ages, which is a problem only because they are totally delicious but not on most diet plans. I decided to keep my calorie count in check by creating my own mini version, and I am happy to report that they are just as good and look much better on my waistline. If you or someone you know has a Chipwich problem, please pass this recipe along—it helps. I know.*

◇◇◇◇◇◇◇◇◇◇◇◇◇◇◇◇◇◇◇◇**MAKES 20 TREATS**◇◇◇◇◇◇◇◇◇◇◇◇◇◇◇◇◇◇◇◇

In a large bowl, whisk together the egg yolks, sugar, vanilla, and salt until completely combined. Set aside.

Heat the evaporated milk in a medium nonstick saucepan over medium heat, stirring constantly, until it comes to a simmer, about 6 minutes. Slowly add the hot milk to the egg yolk mixture, whisking constantly until fully incorporated.

Transfer the mixture back to the saucepan and cook over medium heat, continuing to whisk constantly, until it is thick and custardy, about 5 minutes. Remove from the heat and cool for 15 minutes. Transfer to a clean bowl, cover, and refrigerate for 2 hours until set.

Whip ½ cup of the cream with an electric mixer at medium speed (or use a food processor; see page 105) until soft peaks form, 2 to 3 minutes. Fold the whipped cream into the egg mixture just until all lumps are gone.

CONTINUED

At this point, you've created a delicious vanilla custard. Feel free to serve as you'd like!

Pour the mixture into an ice cube tray and freeze for at least 4 hours, until solid.

Combine the frozen custard cubes and the remaining ¼ cup heavy cream in a food processor and process until smooth, about 30 seconds. Transfer the mixture to a large freezer-safe container and freeze for at least 4 more hours.

You can serve the ice cream as is, or continue to assemble your sandwiches.

Spread 1 tablespoon of the ice cream over the flat side of a cookie and top with another cookie, flat side down. Freeze overnight.

Another good use for the homemade vanilla ice cream from the Baby Ice Cream Sandwiches recipe is in Root Beer Float Shots. Place these little shots on your favorite serving tray and pass them out at your next party.

◇◇◇**MAKES ABOUT 20 1½-OUNCE SERVINGS**◇◇◇

Scoop just under 1 tablespoon ice cream into individual shot glasses. Drizzle hot fudge and whiskey over the ice cream. Top with root beer. Be sure to pour slowly to avoid foam spilling over the edge. Top with a spoonful of whipped cream.

root beer float shots

2 cups vanilla ice cream (see recipe, page 147)

½ cup hot fudge

½ cup whiskey (optional but recommended)

2 cups very cold root beer

2 cups homemade whipped cream (page 105), or store-bought

fruit soup

MY FRIEND ARIELE'S FAMILY *has been making Emeril Lagasse's fruit soup for years. When she first shared the recipe with me on a hot August day, I could practically feel my body temperature go down and instantly craved it. Finally, someone proved that cold soup does not need to involve tomatoes or cucumbers! By using tons of fresh fruits, this may be the least boring and most colorful soup out there. In my adaptation, I've invited some different fruits to the party and cut down the steps required to get there. Simple, easy, delicious,* and *nutritious.*

⬦⬦⬦⬦⬦⬦⬦⬦MAKES ABOUT 20 1½-OUNCE SERVINGS⬦⬦⬦⬦⬦⬦⬦⬦

Heat the ginger in a medium nonstick saucepan over medium-high heat until fragrant, about 2 minutes. Add about half of the chopped strawberries, melon, and mango and the blueberries, along with the lime and orange peels. Stir and cook for another 2 minutes. Add the water, sugar, and orange and lime juices and bring to a simmer, stirring occasionally. Simmer for 5 minutes. Remove from the heat.

Allow the mixture to cool for 10 minutes. Transfer to a food processor. Add the remaining fruit and process until blended, about 1 minute. Transfer to a container, cover, and refrigerate for 1 hour.

Serve in shot glasses or the mini serving vessels of your choice and garnish with lime peel.

CONTINUED

2 tablespoons minced fresh ginger

3 cups hulled and finely chopped strawberries

1 cup finely chopped honeydew melon

2 cups finely chopped mango

1 cup blueberries

2 pieces lime peel, plus more for garnish

2 pieces orange peel

3 cups water

½ cup granulated sugar (optional but recommended)

¼ cup fresh orange juice

2 tablespoons fresh lime juice

The peak season for strawberries is April through June.

The peak season for mangoes is May through September.

The peak season for honeydew is July through August.

The peak season for blueberries is June through August.

If you can't find all of these fruits at the store, feel free to switch them out for other fruits of your liking. The key is buying them fresh.

fruit soup cubes

Take it even further! Pour the fruit soup into ice cube trays or candy molds and freeze for 4 hours. Flex the trays to release the cubes and add a couple to your favorite glasses. Pour champagne over the cubes, and you've got yourself a brunch cocktail.

you can also enjoy thi

flavor combination as a delicious smoothie. Simply double the
ingredients, follow the first step, and serve. It makes about 3 cu

yogurt buttons

POPPING THESE TASTY YOGURT DOTS *into your mouth can be quite addicting—for both kids and adults. But don't worry—this habit is not a problem! Unlike other "once you pop, you can't stop" treats, these are completely healthy. Not to mention, cute as a button.*

¼ cup finely chopped mango

¼ cup fresh blueberries

1 tablespoon fresh lime juice

1½ tablespoons granulated sugar (optional)

1 cup nonfat plain vanilla yogurt (or full fat if you prefer; see box, page 145)

◇◇◇◇◇◇◇◇◇◇◇◇◇◇◇**MAKES ABOUT 75 TREATS**◇◇◇◇◇◇◇◇◇◇◇◇◇◇◇

Combine the mango, blueberries, lime juice, and sugar in a food processor and process until blended, about 1 minute. Add the yogurt and process until smooth, about 1 minute.

Line a cookie sheet with wax paper and set aside.

Pour the blended yogurt mixture into the corner of a large plastic bag. Cut off a tiny piece of the corner of the bag. Squeeze quarter-size dots onto the prepared cookie sheet.

Freeze for 2 hours, then gently remove the buttons from the wax paper and serve immediately.

Add a little bit of food coloring to the yogurt mixture to get different-color buttons. Here are some ideas:

One or two drops of red food coloring will make them pink. After making your buttons, arrange into hearts on your dessert plates and serve for Valentine's Day.

Or separate the mixture into three different bowls. Drop blue food coloring into one bowl and mix. Drop red into another and mix. Leave the third as is. Make your buttons and serve on the Fourth of July.

pudding pops

MY HUSBAND HAS ALWAYS LOVED *Bill Cosby… specifically his Jell-O pudding commercials circa 1987. So random, right? After eating just a spoonful or two of pudding, he can do an* uncanny impression. *When I first told him about this chocolate pudding pop recipe, he couldn't understand why I didn't want to name it "The Cosby." Though Dr. Huxtable didn't make it into the recipe title, his enthusiasm for pudding has definitely resonated in our household. Bill, there is a pop with your name on it waiting in Brooklyn!*

MAKES ABOUT 20 TREATS

In a small saucepan off the heat, combine the sugar and cornstarch. Add the milk and stir until evenly distributed. Place over medium heat, bring to a simmer, and simmer until the mixture begins to thicken, about 5 minutes, stirring occasionally.

Add the chocolate and stir until melted, 1 to 2 minutes. Remove from the heat and stir in the vanilla. Let sit for about 10 minutes.

Spoon the mixture into ice cube trays. Gently tap the trays against a hard surface to even out the mixture. Wrap 2 layers of aluminum foil over the top of the trays. Create holes in the foil by inserting an ice pop stick, blunt side down, into each cube.

Freeze for 4 hours, or until solid. Remove the foil and carefully flex the trays to release the pops.

Don't worry if you don't have ice pop sticks handy. Since the pops are so small, they can be supported with coffee stirrers. Another alternative is very firm straws. These come in all different patterns and are fairly easy to find in the summertime. Any home goods store's outdoor dining section will carry them.

2 tablespoons granulated sugar

1 tablespoon cornstarch

1 cup whole milk

⅓ cup milk or dark chocolate chopped into small pieces

½ teaspoon vanilla extract

10 ice pop sticks, cut in half

Two layers of aluminum foil will help the ice pop sticks stay upright while the pops are freezing.

peach yogurt pops

GF

3 large ripe peaches, peeled and roughly chopped

¼ cup granulated sugar

2 tablespoons fresh lemon juice

2 cups plain whole milk yogurt (see box, page 145)

15 ice pop sticks, cut in half

Peaches are in peak season in July and August, but if you are craving these pops and can't find peaches at the store, feel free to use canned or frozen ones. The pops will still turn out great.

THERE ARE FEW FRUITS SWEETER *than a ripe peach—it's practically a candy that grows on a tree! When you take this summer star and make it into a frozen pop, you're sure to have a treat that will brighten even the sunniest and warmest day of the year.*

◇◇◇◇◇◇◇◇◇◇◇◇◇◇**MAKES ABOUT 30 TREATS**◇◇◇◇◇◇◇◇◇◇◇◇◇◇

Combine the peach pieces, sugar, and lemon juice in a food processor and process until smooth, about 1 minute. Add the yogurt and process until completely smooth, 1 to 2 minutes.

Spoon the mixture into ice cube trays. Gently tap the trays against a hard surface to even out the mixture. Wrap 2 layers of aluminum foil over the top of the trays. Create holes in the foil by inserting an ice pop stick, blunt side down, into each cube.

Freeze for 4 hours, or until solid. Remove the foil and carefully flex the trays to release the pops.

mintamelon pops

RECENTLY I WAS AT *one of my favorite cocktail bars in New York City on one of the hottest, most humid nights of summer. All I wanted—no, needed—was a refreshing drink; per the bartender's recommendation I ordered the aptly named "Cool Down." It was a melon mint julep served with frozen blueberries and a lemon wedge. At first I was a bit skeptical of the flavor combination, as there seemed to be a little too much going on, but I absolutely loved it. And really, what's more refreshing than when things that you never thought would work come together so nicely? It since has become my go-to drink and is the inspiration behind this refreshing pop.*

◇◇◇◇◇◇◇◇◇◇◇◇◇◇**MAKES ABOUT 30 TREATS**◇◇◇◇◇◇◇◇◇◇◇◇◇◇

Combine the watermelon, sugar, and lemon juice in a food processor and process until smooth, about 1 minute. Transfer to a clean bowl and stir in the mint and salt using a spoon or spatula.

Pour the puree into ice cube trays, filling each opening about three-quarters full. Spear 2 blueberries on the end of each ice pop stick using the blunt side. Place each stick into a slot, blueberry side down. They should stand up straight.

Freeze for 4 hours, or until solid. Carefully flex the trays to release the pops.

4 cups roughly cubed watermelon, seeds removed

2 tablespoons granulated sugar

2 teaspoons fresh lemon juice

¼ cup mint leaves, minced

½ teaspoon salt

1 cup fresh or frozen blueberries

15 ice pop sticks, cut in half

rosemary lemonade

THE LEMONADE STAND IS *an establishment that has been around for decades. The one right in front of my childhood home was my first business venture—a precursor to No Bake Makery perhaps—and taught me many entrepreneurial skills ... one of which was the hard lesson of sharing: My cousin took half the profits! Thankfully my friends learned the same lessons as kids—my friend Lizzie shared this recipe with me, and it's one of my faves.*

◇◇◇◇◇◇◇◇◇◇◇**MAKES 20 1½-OUNCE SERVINGS**◇◇◇◇◇◇◇◇◇◇◇

In a medium nonstick saucepan, bring the water to a boil over high heat. Add the rosemary sprigs and dissolve the sugar in the boiling water, stirring constantly, for about 3 minutes. Remove the pan from the heat. Do not allow syrup to boil for more than 2 or 3 minutes or it will become too thick. Strain the simple syrup into a small bowl and cool for 20 minutes.

Combine the ice cubes, vodka, lemon juice, and simple syrup in a food processor or blender and process just until slushy, about 1 minute. Spoon into shot glasses or the mini serving vessels of your choice. Garnish with rosemary and fresh lemon wedges.

½ cup water

Sprigs of 1 fresh rosemary stalk (about ½ cup), plus more for garnish

1 cup granulated sugar

24 ice cubes

1 cup vodka (optional)

6 tablespoons fresh lemon juice

Lemon wedges for garnish

moussies

2 cups bittersweet or semisweet
chocolate chips

1½ cups water

6 tablespoons
granulated sugar

½ teaspoon instant espresso
powder or instant coffee granules

6 large egg whites

2 cups roughly chopped biscotti

⅔ cup chilled heavy cream

2 teaspoons fresh lemon juice

1 teaspoon grated lemon zest

WHILE THE NAME COULD EASILY *be confused with the large mammal from the north or the styling serum we put in our hair, the dessert is quite distinct. The defining characteristic of mousse is its foamy, fluffy texture—in fact, the word* mousse *means "foam" in French. As is true for most French cuisine, achieving the right texture and flavor is no small challenge; many mousse recipes involve vigorous whisking work. Here we've simplified the method, added a little biscotti to complement the espresso flavor, and included a light lemony cream to cut the richness of the chocolate to the perfect level.*

◇◇◇◇◇◇◇◇◇◇◇**MAKES ABOUT 20 1½-OUNCE SERVINGS**◇◇◇◇◇◇◇◇◇◇◇

Place the chocolate in a food processor.

Bring the water, 5 tablespoons of the sugar, and the espresso powder to a simmer in a medium saucepan over medium heat, stirring to dissolve the sugar. Once the sugar is dissolved, quickly transfer the espresso to the food processor and process with the chocolate for about 20 seconds.

Whisk the egg whites in a small bowl, and then add them to the processor and process again for 1 minute.

Transfer the mixture to a large bowl and gently fold in the biscotti pieces. Chill uncovered until firm, about 2 hours.

When the mixture has set, combine the cream, lemon juice, lemon zest, and the remaining 1 tablespoon sugar and beat using an electric mixer at medium speed (or use a food processor; see page 105) until soft peaks form, 2 to 3 minutes.

Layer 1 tablespoon mousse, 1 tablespoon cream, and another tablespoon mousse in shot glasses or the mini serving vessels of your choice.

mini dirt puddings

DIRT PUDDING IS A SIGNATURE *childhood dish—and it makes complete sense. Every child yearns to play with dirt, so the notion of being able to eat it is that much more exciting. Throw in some bright, sugary worms, and you've got a delicious dream in a cup—for all ages! If you haven't eaten dirt pudding since you were a kid, try this out. It's better than you remember.*

◇◇◇◇◇◇◇◇◇◇◇**MAKES ABOUT 20 1½-OUNCE SERVINGS**◇◇◇◇◇◇◇◇◇◇◇

To make the pudding, combine the sugar and cornstarch in a small nonstick saucepan off the heat. Add the milk and stir until evenly distributed. Place over medium heat and bring to a boil; cook until the mixture begins to thicken, about 5 minutes. Add the chocolate and stir until melted, about 1 minute.

Remove from the heat and stir in the vanilla. Transfer to a large clean bowl, place a piece of parchment paper on the surface of the pudding, and refrigerate for at least 4 hours or overnight.

Place the chocolate sandwich cookies in the food processor and process until crumbs form, about 30 seconds. Stir the crumbs into the pudding.

Spoon into shot glasses or the mini serving vessels of your choice and add the gummi worms.

¼ cup granulated sugar

2 tablespoons cornstarch

2 cups skim milk (you can use whole milk for a richer pudding)

⅔ cup milk or dark chocolate chopped into small pieces

1 teaspoon vanilla extract

45 chocolate sandwich cookies (I like Joe-Joes)

20 gummi worms (about 1 medium package)

gelly ceviche

IT'S ABOUT TIME THAT OLD-FASHIONED *1920s ice cream–gelatin dessert got a funky twist. The throwback flavor and texture are always cherished, but the serving style here is much more fun (not to mention easier!) than cutting into a big bulky mold. Just place your serving spoons on a pretty platter before taking out these cold treats and walk them around. This ceviche is a "pinky-up" kind of dessert!*

MAKES ABOUT 30 SERVINGS

In a large bowl, stir the gelatin into the boiling water. Add the ice cream in large spoonfuls, stirring constantly until combined evenly. Stir in the lemon rind.

Refrigerate uncovered for 20 minutes, or until thickened but not quite set. Stir in the strawberries.

Evenly spread the mixture in a 9 by 13-inch glass pan that's about 1 inch deep. Refrigerate for 4 hours, or until firm.

Remove from the refrigerator and use your choice of 1-inch cookie cutters to stamp out bite-size treats. Place the treats on spoons and serve with tiny lemon wedges for squeezing.

If it's extra-hot out, serve these frozen. Follow the same steps as above, but once you've cut or stamped out your bites, place them on a cookie sheet lined with wax paper and freeze for 1 hour before serving.

One 3-ounce package lemon gelatin (I like Jell-O brand)

1¼ cups boiling water

1 pint strawberry ice cream or frozen yogurt

1 teaspoon grated lemon rind

1½ cups finely chopped fresh strawberries

4 lemons, each cut into 8 tiny wedges

Candy AND Cookies

To me, candy and cookies come from the same enticing place of awesomeness, and they have the ability to bring any treat from good to *great*. Take the Sadie (page 101), for example. Yes, a no bake brownie is tasty. But a no bake brownie topped with Reese's Pieces and Twix is undoubtedly better. And how about Mini Dirt Puddings (page 167)? Without the crushed chocolate sandwich cookies and gummi worms there would be no dirt to speak of! Both candy and cookies simply have a playful effect on whatever they touch. There is no such thing as a stuck-up cookie or a highbrow candy; leave that to the crèmes brûlées and soufflés of the world. These guys are for the lighthearted. And of course, the connoisseurs of all things lighthearted are kids.

I challenge you to find a child who hasn't begged for a candy bar or cookie and then behaved well in return. There is a reason candy is the last thing you see at the grocery store checkout counter and cookies are present at the diner cash wrap. They are totally irresistible. And while it is no coincidence that these treats are placed at the eye level of a six-year-old, it does not take a child's convincing for adults to indulge on their own.

Though we may try to deny it, we adults love candy and cookies just as much as we did when we were young. They're a way for us to have fun amid our daily stressors. One of my coworkers, who shall remain nameless, buys *two* Twix bar packs at a time at the vending machine—yep, that's four sticks total. The first time I saw her do it, I was shocked, but upon further reflection, I totally understood. If you're in a stress crunch at the office, you *need* backup candy. Am I wrong? Personally, I am a sucker for anything peanut butter, sweet and sour, salted chocolate and caramel, fruity and gummy, powdered and sugary—which covers most of the bases. In this chapter, you'll get a taste of all that and more. Maybe you'll even be compelled to keep a stash of Hey, Butter Cups (page 180) in the bottom drawer of your desk in case of an emergency.

2¼ cups milk chocolate chopped into quarter-size pieces (or Wilton Candy Melts)

¾ cup Chex cereal

2 tablespoons unsalted butter

½ cup granulated sugar

2 tablespoons evaporated milk

¾ cup marshmallow fluff

2 tablespoons unsalted creamy peanut butter

½ teaspoon vanilla extract

1 cup salted peanuts

Use any variety of Chex except wheat to make this treat gluten-free. Honey nut, rice, corn, and chocolate are all gluten-free!

snickerish

NOW THAT YOU HAVE SUCCESSFULLY *made fudge and caramel (if you are following these recipes sequentially, that is), the time has come for you to conquer the next dessert peak: nougat! The rainbow assortment of candy bars that use nougat is surely a testament to its versatility and deliciousness. The creamy and fluffy texture can be used to enhance a variety of flavor combinations, the most famous of which is the Snickers bar. Snickers are great, but they are a bit too straightforward for me: The caramel-and-nougat combo is just gooey on gooey. Here I decided to re-create all that we love about Snickers but added some extra crunch to make things a bit more interesting.*

◇◇◇◇◇◇◇◇◇◇◇◇◇◇◇◇◇◇**MAKES ABOUT 20 TREATS**◇◇◇◇◇◇◇◇◇◇◇◇◇◇◇◇◇◇

Line an 8 by 8-inch baking sheet with aluminum foil and coat it with nonstick spray. Set aside.

Melt and temper 1 cup of the milk chocolate (or melt Wilton Candy Melts). Pour it along the bottom of the pan and smooth it into an even layer with a rubber spatula. Create a second even layer with the Chex cereal. Place the pan in the freezer for 10 minutes.

To make the nougat, melt the butter in a medium saucepan over medium heat. Add the sugar and evaporated milk, stirring until dissolved, and bring to a low boil. Continue stirring constantly for about 5 minutes, until completely combined. Add the fluff, peanut butter, and vanilla to the pan, stirring until smooth. Remove from the heat and pour the mixture over the Chex layer. Allow to cool completely, about 20 minutes.

Melt and temper the remaining 1¼ cups chocolate (or melt the remaining Wilton Candy Melts) and pour it over the nougat layer. Top with the peanuts. Refrigerate for 45 minutes, or until solid.

Transfer to a cutting board, peel off the foil, and cut into two-bite squares with a sharp knife.

60 saltine crackers

1 cup chocolate-hazelnut spread
(I like Nutella—and so does Nani!)

1½ cups milk chocolate chopped
into quarter-size pieces (or Wilton
Candy Melts)

1 cup sprinkles of your choice

the nani

THIS ONE IS FOR *my precious niece Natalie. She adores Nutella. Every time my sister asks her what she'd like for dinner, she jumps up and down saying "Nutella!" Well, I'm with you, Nani. I'll take a Nutella treat over peas and carrots any night. In fact, sometimes I spread Nutella on saltine crackers— I love the taste of sweet-on-salty. Since I can never eat just one, I decided to stack them into a cookie and seal them with some sprinkles for good measure. I have to keep my eye on these around Nani—they tend to disappear.*

◇◇◇◇◇◇◇◇◇◇◇◇◇◇◇◇**MAKES 20 TREATS**◇◇◇◇◇◇◇◇◇◇◇◇◇◇◇◇

Line a cookie sheet with wax paper.

Place 20 of the saltine crackers flat side up on the prepared cookie sheet. Spread chocolate-hazelnut spread on each cracker and top with another cracker, creating sandwiches. Repeat, adding another layer. Each cookie will have 3 saltines and 2 layers of chocolate-hazelnut spread.

Melt and temper the chocolate (or melt Wilton Candy Melts), and pour it into a shallow bowl. Pour the sprinkles into a separate shallow bowl. If these ingredients don't all fit at once, you can refill or top off the bowls as you continue.

Dip the sides of the cookies first into the milk chocolate and then into the sprinkles, sealing the edges. Refrigerate for 30 minutes, or until solid.

fluffy cracker cookies

I FIRST TASTED THIS COOKIE *at my friend Maggie's dinner party. While we waited for the last of our girlfriends to arrive, she let us have a little taste test— an advantage to arriving early! You know a dessert is irresistible when it gets dipped into before the main course. Maggie explained that her mom had sent her the recipe. She said, "It's just cracker, peanut butter, fluff, cracker, chocolate. That's it." I brought a few home with me that night as a party favor, and though the treats didn't last very long, I never forgot the recipe. How could I?*

MAKES 20 TREATS

Line a cookie sheet with wax paper.

Place all 40 crackers on the prepared cookie sheet flat side up. Spread peanut butter on 20 crackers and fluff on 20 crackers. Place the crackers with the fluff on top of those with the peanut butter, making 20 peanut butter-fluff sandwiches.

Melt and temper the milk chocolate (or melt Wilton Candy Melts). Dip half of each sandwich into the milk chocolate and return to the wax paper. Refrigerate for 45 minutes, or until firm.

Melt and temper the white chocolate (or melt Wilton Candy Melts). Dip the other half of each sandwich into the white chocolate and return to the wax paper. Refrigerate for 45 minutes, or until firm.

40 Ritz crackers

½ cup salted creamy peanut butter

½ cup marshmallow fluff

1½ cups milk chocolate chopped into quarter-size pieces (or Wilton Candy Melts)

1½ cups white chocolate chopped into quarter-size pieces (or Wilton Candy Melts)

If you want to put a little more energy into decorating, there is a great speckled white chocolate candy melt from Wilton that makes these extra cute. You can substitute it for the regular white chocolate. Another great option—always—is sprinkles! Just pour your favorite sprinkles into a shallow bowl; after dipping the second half of your cookie into white chocolate, dip it into sprinkles.

½ cup (1 stick) unsalted butter

2 tablespoons granulated sugar

2 tablespoons packed brown sugar

1 cup chopped salted pecans

2 egg whites

1 teaspoon vanilla extract

2¼ cups crisp rice cereal (I like Rice Krispies)

1 cup powdered sugar

Use Kellogg's Rice Krispies Gluten-Free cereal to make this treat gluten-free.

powder baby

EVERY YEAR FOR CHRISTMAS, *my sister-in-law Brittany bakes the most delicious cookies. They are nutty, crunchy rounds coated with tons of powdered sugar. She presents them in little plastic buckets with a bow on top of the lid. All the powdered sugar in the bucket makes it look like it's filled with snow—and when the bucket is opened, the smells of the vanilla and sugar hit you like a snowball! Inspired, I set out to re-create them, without baking, of course, and so the Powder Baby was born.*

⬦⬦⬦⬦⬦⬦⬦⬦⬦⬦⬦⬦MAKES ABOUT 30 TREATS⬦⬦⬦⬦⬦⬦⬦⬦⬦⬦⬦⬦

Line a cookie sheet with wax paper and set aside.

In a large nonstick saucepan, melt the butter over low heat, about 2 minutes. Remove from the heat and add the granulated sugar, brown sugar, and pecans, mixing well until combined. Return to the heat, add the egg whites, and stir until the ingredients are all melted together, about 4 minutes.

Remove the pan from the heat. Add the vanilla and rice cereal, stirring until combined. Allow to cool for 15 minutes.

Scoop out 1-inch clusters with a rounded tablespoon or cookie scoop and place on the prepared cookie sheet. Refrigerate for 30 minutes.

Use your hands to round out the shape of the cookies and roll each through powdered sugar before serving.

2/3 cup salted creamy peanut butter

3 tablespoons unsalted butter

3 tablespoons firmly packed light brown sugar

2/3 cup powdered sugar

2¼ cups dark or milk chocolate chopped into quarter-size pieces (or Wilton Candy Melts)

Sea salt (optional)

hey, butter cup

I TAKE A LOT OF PRIDE in being able to craft innovative desserts, but sometimes there are treats so simple and so perfect that no change is needed. The peanut butter cup definitely falls into that category, best enjoyed in its most pure form. But making these little cups on your own will make you feel like you've really earned them—and you'll enjoy them even more.

MAKES 24 TREATS

Line a mini muffin tin with paper liners and set aside. Line a cookie sheet with wax paper and set aside.

In a medium saucepan over medium heat, stir together the peanut butter, butter, and brown sugar. Once the mixture is completely melted and begins to bubble lightly, remove from the heat. Add the powdered sugar 1 tablespoon at a time, stirring until smooth. Let sit until cool enough to handle, about 5 minutes.

Melt and temper 1 cup of the chocolate (or melt 1 cup Wilton Candy Melts), and pour just enough into each muffin cup to cover its bottom. Tap the tin gently against a hard surface to even out the chocolate. Refrigerate for about 30 minutes.

Roll the peanut butter mixture into teaspoon-size balls, using your hands, and place on the prepared cookie sheet, spacing evenly. They may flatten immediately, depending on how warm your mixture is. If they don't, use your hands or a rubber spatula to flatten the balls into disks about ½ inch thick. Refrigerate for 20 minutes.

To assemble your peanut butter cups, place one peanut butter disk on top of each chocolate-coated liner, making sure to leave room on the sides and top of the cups.

Melt and temper the remaining 1¼ cups chocolate (or melt the remaining Wilton Candy Melts), and pour it on top of the peanut butter filling. Once again, tap the tin gently against a hard surface to even out the chocolate. Refrigerate for 30 minutes, or until solid. Sprinkle with salt, if using.

popcorn balls

POPCORN IS A PERFECTLY CRUNCHY *canvas for a variety of flavors. From rosemary to curry to cheddar to caramel, popcorn embraces whatever you throw at it. And with the right sticky agent, it can take on a different shape—making half-inch pieces of popped corn into a two-inch ball. Let's face it—most of us put about that much of it in our mouths at once anyway.*

MAKES ABOUT 20 TREATS

Line a baking sheet with parchment or wax paper and set aside.

Pour the ice water into a medium bowl. Place the popcorn in a large bowl.

Combine the brown sugar, corn syrup, and butter in a small saucepan. Place over medium heat and bring to a low boil, stirring constantly. Continue to stir until the sugar is dissolved, 2 to 3 minutes. If you are using a thermometer, it should read 245 to 250°F. Remove from the heat and stir in the salt, cinnamon, and nutmeg.

For a chocolate variety, substitute 1½ tablespoons cocoa powder for the cinnamon and nutmeg.

Pour the mixture evenly over the popcorn. Mix well with a rubber spatula, ensuring that the popcorn is coated evenly.

Dip both your hands into the ice water. Work quickly to press small handfuls of the popcorn mixture firmly into 2-inch balls and place the balls on the prepared baking sheet. Continue to dip your hands into the water as necessary while you're making the balls. Let cool for 15 to 20 minutes before serving.

½ cup ice water

6 cups plain popped corn (about 2½ standard bags)

⅓ cup packed light brown sugar

¼ cup light corn syrup

2 tablespoons unsalted butter

½ teaspoon salt

½ teaspoon ground cinnamon

½ teaspoon ground nutmeg

If you don't have a candy thermometer, you can tell your sugar is ready by dropping a small amount (about ½ teaspoon) into very cold water. If it forms a ball that holds its shape but is still sticky when pressed with your fingers, it's ready!

caramelly in my belly

THESE TASTY TREATS TURN OUT *like coins, similar to the ones you find during the holidays that come in gold nets wrapped in gold foil. I'm talking about gelt, a staple of Hanukkah traditions. But we don't need any gold to show the value of these—the sea salt and crystallized sugar give them the tiniest crunch and a sparkle all on their own.*

◇◇◇◇◇◇◇◇◇◇◇◇◇◇◇◇◇◇◇**MAKES ABOUT 30 TREATS**◇◇◇◇◇◇◇◇◇◇◇◇◇◇◇◇◇◇◇

Line a cookie sheet with wax paper and set aside.

To make the caramel, cook the sugar in a small saucepan over low-medium heat until it forms a dark liquid and begins to bubble, 6 to 7 minutes. Add the lemon juice and stir. Slowly pour the cream over the mixture and stir until the caramelized sugar is dissolved into the cream. Immediately remove from the heat.

Melt and temper the chocolate (or melt Wilton Candy Melts) and transfer to a medium bowl. Pour the hot caramel mixture over the melted chocolate and immediately stir with a spatula until combined.

Drop the mixture by the ½ teaspoon onto the prepared cookie sheet. Allow to sit at room temperature until firm but not completely solid (about 10 minutes); then top each portion with a sprinkle of salt and crystallized sugar.

Cover with another sheet of wax paper and gently press a second cookie sheet onto the chocolate coins to flatten. Refrigerate until solid, about 1 hour. Deposit the coins into your belly!

1 tablespoon granulated sugar

½ teaspoon lemon juice

¼ cup heavy cream

1½ cups milk chocolate chopped into quarter-size pieces (or Wilton Candy Melts)

1 teaspoon sea salt

2 tablespoons crystallized sugar (your choice of color)

If you don't have a second cookie sheet to flatten your coins with, don't worry. Just use a plate, cutting board, book, or any other heavy, flat object that you don't mind refrigerating.

birds' nests

2 tablespoons unsalted butter

4 cups mini marshmallows

¼ cup salted creamy
peanut butter

¼ cup dark chocolate chips

4 cups chow mein noodles,
roughly chopped

1 cup mini jelly beans

WHEN I WAS IN COLLEGE *I was a member of the Big Sister Association of Boston, a mentoring program in which women are paired up with little girls from troubled backgrounds. Initially I had some difficulty getting my six-year-old "little sister" to open up to me, so I pulled out all the tricks—watercolors, nail polish, cupcakes, you name it. A few months into the program, we met on the Monday after Easter. I brought these Birds' Nests as a treat, and so vividly I remember her saying, "Are you sure I can eat this?" I assured her they were meant for eating, and she responded, "But they are so cute!" With a little encouragement, she picked out all the pink jelly beans and finally gave the nest a little nibble. She immediately started giggling and then finished it off. Of all the things I had tried,* that moment was our breakthrough.

MAKES ABOUT 25 TREATS

Line a cookie sheet with wax paper and set aside.

In a large nonstick saucepan, melt the butter over medium heat. Add the marshmallows and stir until melted, about 3 minutes. Add the peanut butter and chocolate chips and stir until the ingredients are distributed evenly.

Remove from the heat. Stir the chow mein noodles into the mixture until completely coated. Transfer to a medium bowl and let sit until just cool enough to handle, about 3 minutes. If the mixture cools too long, it will harden.

Using your hands, roll the mixture into 1-inch balls. Flatten the balls into disks and place on the prepared cookie sheet. Use your thumb to indent the middle of the nests, and fill each nest with 3 or 4 jelly beans.

the chu
(fruit leather)

MY ADORABLE NIECE AMANDA'S NICKNAME *is Chuchi—I call her Chu for short. My sister used to baby talk to her, speaking nonsense, as we all do with newborns. Every time she said the meaningless word chuchi! my niece would giggle so hard that eventually it stuck and became her nickname. And Chu loves chewy fruit roll snacks, just like I did when I was five. She is always chewin' on those things! Their sticky texture makes them seem like one of those super-complicated, can-only-be-purchased snacks, but they are actually super-easy to make at home. This chew's for Chu!*

◇◇◇◇◇◇◇◇◇◇◇◇◇◇**MAKES ABOUT 30 SERVINGS**◇◇◇◇◇◇◇◇◇◇◇◇◇◇

Place the pears, strawberries, and sugar in a food processor or blender and process until smooth, about 1 minute.

Pour the fruit puree into a medium nonstick saucepan and bring to a low boil over medium heat; boil until the mixture is reduced by half, about 6 minutes. Remove from the heat and let sit for 5 minutes.

Coat a large microwave-safe plate or pan with nonstick spray. Evenly spread the mixture over the surface of the plate, making sure the edges are not too thin (otherwise they will burn). Microwave on medium power for about 5 minutes, until the leather is no longer sticky in the center. If more cooking time is needed, continue to cook on medium power in 30-second intervals, watching closely to ensure that the leather does not burn.

Repeat the process with the remaining fruit puree. Let stand at room temperature uncovered overnight to dry. Cut into two-bite strips and roll up. Chew!

4 pears, peeled and roughly chopped

2 cups strawberries, roughly chopped

2½ tablespoons sugar

sour lemon-lime gummies

THOUGH SMELL IS USUALLY THE *best indicator of the appeal of a treat (or any food for that matter), in some rare cases, a simple sound will suffice. These gummi candies most certainly fall into that category. When you hear that lip-smacking sound, you'll know you have a winner on your hands—sweet and sour and totally irresistible.*

2 cups water

⅔ cup lemonade drink mix (I like Kool-Aid)

½ cup lime flavor gelatin (I like Jell-O brand)

6 tablespoons unflavored gelatin (found in the baking section of your grocery store; I like Knox brand)

⅔ cup granulated sugar (optional)

◇◇◇◇◇◇◇◇◇◇◇◇◇◇◇**MAKES ABOUT 30 TREATS**◇◇◇◇◇◇◇◇◇◇◇◇◇◇◇

Very lightly coat an ice cube tray with nonstick spray and set aside.

Pour the water into a medium saucepan; place over medium heat and bring to a boil. Add the drink mix and the lime and unflavored gelatins; immediately stir until all the powder is dissolved. Remove from the heat.

Pour the mixture into a measuring cup, then into the prepared tray, filling each about halfway. Refrigerate for 20 minutes, or until set.

Carefully flex the ice cube trays to release the candies. You may need to use a small spoon to lift the corners of the candy out of each slot to remove them.

If using, pour the sugar into a shallow bowl and roll the candy through the sugar.

Feel free to mix and match drink mix and gelatin flavors to your liking! They come in strawberry, melon, kiwi—you name it.

Breakfast
FOR
Dessert

Mini Churros

Pancake Bites

Apple Donut Holes

Caramel Crumble

Granola Squares

French Toast Sticks

Oatmeal Chewies

Tiny Ricotta Crepes

As happens to most, upon graduating from high school, my three best friends and I sadly parted ways for college. Thankfully, two of us went to one school and two to another, meaning only two visits had to be made each year. Lorelle and I went to Boston University, where there is no football team and the school buildings are integrated with the city. Sarah and Christina went to the University of Florida, where you can practically smell the school spirit in the air. And that school spirit came along with the one thing that made Christina and Sarah different from Lorelle and me: sororities.

Having heard the bizarre rush stories and all kinds of Greek gossip, we arrived for our first visit to UF skeptical of our friends' new lives, to say the least. What in the world does this story have to do with Breakfast for Dessert, you ask? Well, there was one thing that changed our cynical viewpoint of sorority life, and that, my friends, was a night called "Breakfast for Dinner." The entire house gathered together around 6 p.m. in the dining room and had pancakes, eggs, muffins—any and every breakfast delight was at the ready. After that meal, we really started to warm up to the sorority and the girls in it. How could you *not* want to eat breakfast at night with all your girlfriends?

Since then, I make eggs and bacon for dinner all the time. But over time, I also took it a step further and began making breakfast for dessert! French toast, pancakes— I'm not sure when in history these super-sweet dishes became meals for first thing in the morning. At first glance it may seem odd to serve breakfast for dessert. But, really, I think we should be asking the opposite question: Why are so many desserts served for breakfast? Donuts, danishes, coffee cake, cinnamon rolls...it seems a mystery that these sugary morsels made their way into the most important meal of the day. Don't you think a donut's sister is a cake? And a pancake...I mean, it has the word *cake in it*. I decided it was time to return these treats to the appropriate category, even sweetening them up a little bit extra, and, of course, making them just two bites—which, let's be honest, is really all we need. In fact, just recently I was at brunch with Lorelle, Christina, and Sarah, and someone said, "I really want the pancakes, but just like two bites." Problem solved.

mini churros

OF ALL THE TREATS OUT THERE, *churros are one of the hardest to buy. Why? Because every opportunity you have to get them is embarrassing. In New York City they sell them on the subway platforms, and in Miami they are sold on the side of the road. These underground and aboveground treats come along with some dirtiness and illegality, which causes most people to stay away. While I am sure these makeshift operations offer delicious treats, do you really want to be caught buying one and risk running into your coworker or being seen by your crush? I think not. Go ahead and make these churro-inspired treats at home and save yourself the shame of a public churro purchase. These little treats are so quick, so simple, and you can make them with ingredients you probably already have in the kitchen.*

5 small flour tortillas (fajita size)

½ tablespoon ground cinnamon

1 tablespoon granulated sugar

½ cup vegetable oil

◇◇◇◇◇◇◇◇◇◇◇◇◇◇◇◇◇MAKES ABOUT 50 TREATS◇◇◇◇◇◇◇◇◇◇◇◇◇◇◇

Line a cookie sheet with 3 to 5 layers of paper towels and set aside.

Cut the tortillas in half, then into ½-inch strips. You should be able to get approximately 10 strips out of each tortilla.

Combine the cinnamon and sugar in a large zip-top plastic bag.

Heat the oil in a large, deep pan over medium-high heat until the temperature reaches between 350 and 365°F (see tip at right). Add a few strips at once, leaving about ½ inch between them. Fry, flipping once. Remove from the pan when golden on both sides (15 to 20 seconds total if your oil is at the right temperature). Remove the strips from the pan using tongs (or 2 dinner forks) and place on the prepared cookie sheet. Repeat until all the strips have been fried.

Place the strips into the zip-top bag, seal it, and shake it all around until the churros are completely coated.

The ideal oil temperature for frying is between 350 and 365°F. If you do not have a cooking thermometer, no worries. Just stick the end of a wooden spoon into the oil. If you see bubbles form around the wood and start to float up, your oil is hot enough to cook with.

Be *very careful*—hot oil is dangerous, but you need it to be this temperature, because the hotter the oil, the less of it the strips will absorb.

pancake bites

PANCAKES

¾ cup whole milk (reduced-fat is okay too)

1 tablespoon white vinegar

1 cup all-purpose flour

2 tablespoons granulated sugar

1 teaspoon baking powder

½ teaspoon baking soda

½ teaspoon salt

2 tablespoons unsalted butter

1 large egg

½ cup mini chocolate chips

FROSTING

4 ounces cream cheese, softened (I recommend using light or ⅓ fat)

½ cup powdered sugar

½ teaspoon vanilla extract

HAVE YOU EVER MET SOMEONE *who doesn't like pancakes? Think about it. Just the mention of a triple-decker stack of flapjacks smothered in butter and maple syrup makes even the driest mouths water. Despite all of their glories, though, pancakes are not the most visually interesting of foods. Why not turn up the sophistication and make this sweetie even sweeter with homemade frosting! I know—I had to see it to believe it too.*

MAKES ABOUT 15 TREATS

Line a cookie sheet with paper towels and set aside.

Mix the milk with the vinegar in a medium bowl and let sit for 5 minutes. This mixture is your "soured" milk.

In a large bowl, combine the flour, sugar, baking powder, baking soda, and salt.

Place the butter in a small bowl and microwave on medium power for about 15 seconds, until melted. Whisk the egg and melted butter into the "soured" milk. Pour the dry ingredients into the wet ingredients and whisk until there are no lumps remaining.

Coat a large skillet with nonstick cooking spray and place over medium heat. Drop teaspoons of batter onto the pan, forming 1-inch rounds. Immediately place a few chocolate chips evenly on each round. When a few bubbles begin to form on top of the pancakes, turn them over using a rubber spatula and continue to cook briefly, about 20 seconds.

CONTINUED

I know putting vinegar in milk sounds kinda funky, but it helps give the pancakes a nice fluffy rise. Don't worry—no one will be able to taste it.

Place the pancakes on the prepared cookie sheet to cool. Repeat until all the batter is used.

To make the frosting, using an electric mixer or whisk, beat the cream cheese, powdered sugar, and vanilla until completely combined and smooth.

Once the pancakes have cooled (about 30 minutes), spread the frosting on two thirds of them. Then assemble your stacks: pancake, frosting, pancake, frosting, pancake. Stick a toothpick in the middle of each and serve.

Between batches, remove your skillet from the heat and clean it with a wet paper towel. Re-grease before starting again. This will help keep your pancakes looking clean and prevent burning.

apple donut holes

THERE IS SOMETHING ABOUT THE DONUT *that makes it seem impossible to conquer. Donuts usually aren't a homemade breakfast choice on a Saturday morning but rather an on-the-go treat when you're late for a meeting. Well, it's time to give the coffee shops a run for their money and make donuts at home! Don't you want to feel that certain sense of victory for cracking the code? These are particularly satisfying; the apple, cinnamon, and nutmeg make them a perfect partner to a cup of (homemade!) coffee on a fall day.*

MAKES ABOUT 25 TREATS

Line a cookie sheet with 3 layers of paper towels and set aside.

Heat 2 cups of the oil in a deep fryer (a heavy saucepan or wok will work too) to between 350 and 365°F (see tip, page 195).

Sift the flour, baking powder, baking soda, cinnamon, nutmeg, and salt into a large bowl. In a medium mixing bowl, combine the granulated sugar, brown sugar, and egg; using a whisk or an electric mixer at medium speed, beat until fluffy. Beat in the remaining 1 tablespoon of oil until combined.

Stir about a tablespoon of the dry ingredients into the egg mixture; then stir in 1 tablespoon of the milk. Repeat until all the ingredients have been combined (beginning and ending with dry ingredients), stirring until well blended.

Stir in the applesauce and apple juice. The batter will become very loose.

CONTINUED

2 cups plus 1 tablespoon vegetable oil

1⅛ cups all-purpose flour

¾ teaspoon baking powder

¼ teaspoon baking soda

½ teaspoon ground cinnamon

½ teaspoon ground nutmeg

⅛ teaspoon salt

¼ cup granulated sugar

2 tablespoons firmly packed light brown sugar

1 large egg

2 tablespoons whole milk

4½ tablespoons unsweetened applesauce

2 tablespoons apple juice or apple cider

½ cup powdered sugar

Don't be alarmed if some of your donuts don't turn out perfectly. It is common that some end up with a tail of sorts—what I call "alien donuts." Personally, I like a donut with some character. You can either use a knife to cut the imperfections off or play the flaws off as intentional and call them donut handles.

Carefully drop the batter by the tablespoon into the hot oil. To prevent overcrowding and uneven cooking, make just 3 or 4 drops at a time. Fry the donuts to cook, turning once with tongs (or 2 dinner forks), for 2 to 3 minutes, until golden. Transfer to the prepared sheet. Allow to cool completely and drain. You may need to refresh with clean paper towels.

Pour the powdered sugar into a couple of brown paper lunch bags. Place the donuts in the bags, grip them shut, and shake well. Fold over the sides of the bags to serve, or transfer the donut holes to plates.

donut pops!

25 (not sugar-dusted) donut holes (page 199), cooled

2½ cups dark chocolate chopped into quarter-size pieces (or Wilton Candy Melts)

25 cake pop or lollipop sticks

1 cup sprinkles (your choice of color)

Take this recipe a step further and make the cake pop's tasty cousin: the donut pop! Donut pops are easy to make and are a surefire hit at any party. There is something about the convenience of treats on a stick that people just love.

MAKES ABOUT 25 TREATS

Line a cookie sheet with wax paper. Place the donut holes on the prepared sheet and refrigerate for 2 hours.

Pour the sprinkles into a shallow bowl and set aside.

Melt and temper the chocolate (or melt Wilton Candy Melts). Dip the tip of the lollipop sticks in the melted chocolate. Push each stick two thirds through a cold donut hole. Dip each pop into the melted chocolate and allow any excess chocolate to drip. Place back on the prepared sheet, stick pointing up; then sprinkle with sprinkles. Refrigerate for 30 minutes, or until solid.

caramel crumble

MANHATTAN IS HOME TO *a famous dessert bar called the Milk Bar, owned by David Chang of Momofuku fame. In fact, Milk Bar opened up shop in Brooklyn as well. I like to think that everything that passes the "New York test" makes its way over to Brooklyn—leaving us with only the most fantastic and original stuff. Along with Milk Bar's famous cakes, truffles, and yogurts, they also have an aptly named "crack pie." It's a caramelly, crumbly number that is totally irresistible. One night before Milk Bar set up shop in Brooklyn, I needed a crack pie fix and created this similarly flavored no bake crumble. Now, with Milk Bar down the street, I've tasted our versions back-to-back and can say with confidence they* both *pass the "New York test" with flying flavors.*

◇◇◇◇◇◇◇◇◇◇◇◇**MAKES ABOUT 20 SERVINGS**◇◇◇◇◇◇◇◇◇◇◇

Line an 8 by 8-inch baking pan with aluminum foil and set aside.

To make the crust, melt 1 tablespoon of the butter in a medium skillet over medium heat. Add the oats and cook, stirring constantly, until lightly toasted, about 2 minutes. Transfer to a clean bowl and cool slightly. Place the wafers and cooled oats in a food processor and process until fine crumbs form.

In the same skillet, combine the remaining 9 tablespoons of butter and the brown sugar; place over medium heat and stir constantly until melted and smooth. Remove from the heat. Stir in the wafer and oat crumbs, salt, and vanilla. Reserve half the mixture for the crumble topping and press the remaining half into the bottom of the prepared pan. Refrigerate until firm, about 30 minutes.

To make the filling, combine the sugar, corn syrup, water, lemon juice, and salt in a 2-cup microwave-safe glass measuring cup or medium glass bowl. Microwave on high power until the mixture begins to take

CRUST AND CRUMBLE LAYERS

10 tablespoons unsalted butter

1½ cups quick-cooking rolled oats (I like Quaker)

45 vanilla wafers (I like Nilla Wafers)

½ cup packed brown sugar

½ teaspoon salt

½ teaspoon vanilla extract

CARAMEL FILLING

1 cup granulated sugar

2 tablespoons light corn syrup

2 tablespoons water

⅛ teaspoon lemon juice

¼ teaspoon salt

½ cup heavy cream

1 tablespoon unsalted butter

CONTINUED

on a caramel color, 4 to 7 minutes, depending on your microwave (begin to check after 4 minutes). Let cool for 5 minutes; the caramel will continue to darken.

While the caramel mixture is cooling, heat the cream in a small non-stick saucepan over medium heat until it comes to a low boil, about 2 minutes. Add the hot cream to the caramel, a few tablespoons at a time. It will bubble up intensely but shouldn't overflow. Add the butter and stir until melted and smooth. Let cool for 5 minutes.

Remove the crust from the refrigerator and evenly pour the caramel over it. Sprinkle the reserved crumb mixture over the caramel; pat down lightly. Freeze until firm, about 1 hour.

Transfer to a cutting board, peel off the foil, and cut into two-bite squares with a sharp knife.

granola squares

WHEN I WAS GROWING UP, *my mom packed a granola bar in my lunch box almost every day—they were and still are one of my favorite snacks. It was one of the only items (sorry, Mom!) that I didn't trade off with my classmates. With such a variety of flavors, I was always torn about which one I liked best. As a kid, my favorite was chocolate. Now it would be a hybrid between oatmeal raisin and nuts with honey. Well, actually, now I don't have to choose because I can make them exactly how I want them at home. If you love these crunchy treats as much as I do, take a stab at making them yourself—just the way you like them.*

MAKES ABOUT 20 SERVINGS

Line an 8 by 8-inch baking pan with plastic wrap and set aside.

If your granola is very clumpy, process it in a food processor until pea-size, about 10 seconds. Be sure not to overprocess, as you don't want a powdery consistency.

Combine the granola, walnuts, raisins, cranberries, and salt in a large bowl and stir until the ingredients are distributed evenly.

Combine the butter, sugar, cinnamon, and honey in a small nonstick saucepan. Place over medium heat and bring to a low boil, stirring occasionally, 4 to 5 minutes. Remove from the heat and stir into the granola mixture until evenly coated. Let sit until cool enough to handle, about 10 minutes.

Place the mixture in the prepared pan and use a rubber spatula to press down firmly and evenly. Refrigerate for 30 minutes.

Transfer to a cutting board, peel away the plastic wrap, and cut into 1-inch squares.

CONTINUED

2½ cups granola (your choice of flavor)

1½ cups salted chopped walnuts

½ cup raisins

½ cup dried cranberries

½ teaspoon salt

6 tablespoons unsalted butter

¾ cup firmly packed brown sugar

2 teaspoons ground cinnamon

½ cup honey

Use a gluten-free granola brand like Udi's or Bakery on Main to make this treat gluten-free.

Feel free to replace the walnuts with any nut of your choosing. Same goes for the raisins and cranberries—they can be swapped out for virtually any dried fruit and even chocolate or peanut butter chips. Without the confines of prepackaging, the possibilities are endless.

french toast sticks

OF ALL THE MEMORIES *I have of the kitchen while growing up, making French toast has to be one of the most visceral. The sound of a cracking egg. My arm getting tired from whisking the batter. The flop of the wet bread when it hits the pan. The sizzle of the eggs firming up over the heat. And finally, the smell of something a little bit savory and a whole lot sweet. French toast is way more than just breakfast—it's an experience. And it's definitely a treat.*

◇◇◇◇◇◇◇◇◇◇◇◇◇**MAKES ABOUT 20 SERVINGS**◇◇◇◇◇◇◇◇◇◇◇◇◇

In a large, shallow bowl, whisk together the eggs, milk, vanilla, honey, and cinnamon.

Using a bread knife, cut the challah into 1-inch-thick slices. Dip each slice of challah into the egg mixture, turning it over once (10 to 15 seconds per side). Each slice should be soaked through but not dripping.

Heat 2 tablespoons of the butter in a large sauté pan over medium heat. Add the soaked bread to the sauté pan and cook for 2 to 3 minutes on each side, until golden brown. Remove from the pan and cool for about 2 minutes.

Cut each cooked French toast slice into long 1-inch-thick strips (the number of strips each slice yields will depend on the size of your challah). Heat the remaining 1 tablespoon butter in the same pan. Place the strips on the pan with one of the uncooked sides down. Cook for 1 to 2 minutes on each uncooked side, flipping to cook each uncooked side until all four sides are golden brown.

Serve hot with maple syrup, fruit, or powdered sugar (see tip, page 41)—or all of the above!

3 large eggs

¾ cup whole milk (reduced-fat is okay too)

¼ teaspoon pure vanilla extract

1 teaspoon honey

Dash of cinnamon

½ large loaf challah bread

3 tablespoons unsalted butter

Maple syrup, fruit, and/or powdered sugar for serving

oatmeal chewies

BEFORE EMBARKING ON MAKING THIS *delicious treat, it's best to measure all your ingredients and place them in separate bowls. You have to work quickly with this recipe, and doing this will make that much easier. Plus, having all of your ingredients measured and lined up will make you feel oh-so-professional. This technique is called* mise en place, *which means "everything in place" in French. In restaurant kitchens, there is a dedicated person for just this task. I remember the first time I practiced mise en place at home—my husband walked into the kitchen and said, "Okay, this is getting serious." While the technique may seem quite businesslike, these Chewies are nothing but easy and fun.*

◆◆◆◆◆◆◆◆◆◆MAKES ABOUT 20 TREATS◆◆◆◆◆◆◆◆◆◆

¼ cup skim or 1% milk

⅓ cup granulated sugar

1 heaping tablespoon cocoa powder

1 teaspoon vanilla extract

5 tablespoons salted creamy peanut butter

1½ cups quick-cooking rolled oats (I like Quaker)

⅓ cup dark chocolate chopped into quarter-size pieces

3 tablespoons sprinkles or nonpareils

Line a cookie sheet with wax paper and set aside.

Combine the milk, sugar, and cocoa powder in a medium nonstick pan; place over medium heat and bring to a boil, 3 to 4 minutes, stirring constantly. Turn off the heat and stir in the vanilla and peanut butter until the peanut butter has melted completely. Pour in the oats and stir until the ingredients are distributed evenly.

Using a rounded tablespoon or cookie scoop, spoon out 1-inch clusters and drop them onto the prepared sheet. Let cool for 10 minutes; then use your hands to perfect their shape. Refrigerate for 2 hours.

Prepare the chocolate for drizzling. Drizzle the chocolate over the Chewies and top with sprinkles or nonpareils. Refrigerate for 20 minutes for the chocolate to harden before serving.

Use Bob's Red Mill gluten-free oats to make this treat gluten-free.

CONTINUED

the berty

2 cups quick-cooking rolled oats
(I like Quaker)

4 heaping tablespoons salted
creamy peanut butter or
almond butter

Sugar-free jam

This heart-healthier version of the Oatmeal Chewies was created by my sister for her husband, Bert, whose sweet tooth and heart condition appreciate this version of the treat. These are good and good for you.

MAKES ABOUT 30 TREATS

Line a cookie sheet with wax paper and set aside.

In a medium bowl, knead the oats with the peanut butter to form a dough. Using a rounded tablespoon or cookie scoop, spoon out 1-inch clusters and place them on the prepared sheet. Use your hands to perfect their shape. Refrigerate for 2 hours.

Remove from refrigerator and dollop the jam on top before serving.

tiny ricotta crepes

ONE OF MY GO-TO LUNCH SPOTS *growing up in Miami was a hole-in-the-wall called the Crepe Maker. And boy, do they make crepes. They have everything from Philly cheesesteak crepes to banana split crepes. But even with all the exciting and innovative options, I would always go for a simple ricotta and fruit filling (an off-the-menu choice). My family surprised me by having the Crepe Maker set up shop at my engagement party—I was the happiest girl ever to hold a crepe in a white party dress. Guess what I ordered?*

MAKES ABOUT 25 SERVINGS

Line a cookie sheet with wax paper and set aside.

To make the filling, combine the ricotta, lemon juice, raspberries, and sugar in a medium bowl. Smash the raspberries with a spatula to break them up into the mixture. Cover and refrigerate for 30 minutes.

To make the crepe batter, in a large bowl, whisk together the flour and eggs. Pour in the milk by the tablespoon, stirring constantly until combined. Repeat with the water.

CONTINUED

½ cup part-skim ricotta cheese

1 tablespoon fresh lemon juice

½ cup raspberries

2 teaspoons granulated sugar

1 cup all-purpose flour

2 large eggs

½ cup whole milk

½ cup water, at room temperature

2 tablespoons unsalted butter

Pinch of salt

½ teaspoon vanilla extract

Powdered sugar for sprinkling (optional)

Place the butter in a small microwave-safe bowl and microwave on medium power for about 15 seconds, until melted. Add the melted butter, salt, and vanilla to the flour mixture and stir until smooth.

Coat a skillet with nonstick spray and heat over medium heat. Use a level tablespoon to drop the batter onto the pan. If you are working with a standard-size pan, you should be able to cook 4 crepes at a time. Be sure to drop them in from opposite ends of the pan—the mixture is loose and will expand quickly.

Cook for about 2 minutes total, until lightly browned, turning once with a rubber spatula. Place the finished crepes on the prepared sheet and cool for 15 minutes.

Spoon the ricotta mixture into the mini crepes and fold over once. Seal with a toothpick if necessary. Sprinkle with powdered sugar if desired (see tip, page 41).

acknowledgments

First, I'd like to thank Judy Linden, my champion of an agent. If she hadn't come across my little blog, this book would not exist. From start to finish, she has made sure my vision came true and for that I am forever grateful.

Thank you to the brilliant team at Grand Central Publishing for giving me this opportunity, especially my editor, Amanda Englander. Her patience, wit, and attention to detail made every single page of this book better. A special thank-you to Jamie Raab, Emi Battaglia, Nick Small, Jane Lee, Toni Marotta, and Carolyn Kurek for their fantastic support, Leda Scheintaub for her keen copyediting, Terri Peck for her patient recipe testing, Brianna Brown for her photo editing, Natalie Sélavy for her styling help, and Liz Connor and Alissa Faden for designing such a cutie of a book.

A big thank-you to Kristen Melega at Fishs Eddy and the generous staff at ABC Kitchen, Les Toiles du Soleil, Anthropologie, Crate & Barrel, and Alessi for loaning me your gorgeous tableware and linens.

A warm thank-you to my wonderful friends, specifically Ariele Fredman for her enthusiasm and help; Kate Dresser and Emilia Pisani for their fantastic "frienditor" skills; Lorelle Kahn, Sarah Rochman, and Christina Oshan for being the best besties ever; Alex Arnold for pointing out all the gluten-free treats in the book; and everyone else who shared ideas, tested recipes, and made this project so much fun.

I am so grateful to my rock of a family for their constant encouragement. Brittany, Toti, Pupi, Bert, Aly, and Dad: you are all wonderful. I am especially thankful to my mom, whose love and support, every day of my life, have inspired me to be a better person and follow my dreams.

And finally, there really are no words to express my appreciation for my wonderful husband and gifted photographer, Jeremy Krumsick. Thank you for being my best friend, biggest fan, and unfailing supporter. I am tremendously lucky to share my life with you. You, truly, are what makes my life sweet.

kitchen & metrics conversions chart

US DRY VOLUME MEASUREMENTS

MEASURE	EQUIVALENT
1/16 teaspoon	a dash
1/8 teaspoon	a pinch
3 teaspoons	1 tablespoon
1/8 cup	2 tablespoons (equal to 1 standard coffee scoop)
1/4 cup	4 tablespoons
1/3 cup	5 tablespoons plus 1 teaspoon
1/2 cup	8 tablespoons
3/4 cup	12 tablespoons
1 cup	16 tablespoons
1 pound	16 ounces

US LIQUID VOLUME MEASUREMENTS

MEASURE	EQUIVALENT
4 ounces	1/2 cup
8 ounces	1 cup
1 pint	2 cups (equal to 16 ounces)
1 quart	2 pints (equal to 4 cups)

US TO METRIC CONVERSIONS

MEASURE	EQUIVALENT
⅕ teaspoon	1 milliliter
1 teaspoon	5 milliliters
1 tablespoon	15 milliliters
1 fluid ounce	30 milliliters
⅕ cup	50 milliliters
1 cup	240 milliliters
2 cups (1 pint)	470 milliliters
4 cups (1 quart)	.95 liter
4 quarts	3.8 liters
1 ounce	28 grams
1 pound	454 grams

FOOD RATIOS

BUTTER			
1 stick	4 ounces = 113 grams	8 tablespoons	½ cup
4 sticks	16 ounces = 452 grams	32 tablespoons	2 cups

CHOCOLATE	
1 ounce	¼ cup grated = 40 grams
6 ounces chips	1 cup chips = 160 grams
cocoa powder	1 cup = 115 grams

index

about the author

CRISTINA SUAREZ KRUMSICK is the chef and proprietor of No Bake Makery. Based in her Brooklyn apartment, she launched her two-bite sweets business in 2011 with nothing but a blog, a PayPal account, and a bunch of no bake recipes. With an active social media presence, Daily Candy feature, and follow-her-dreams attitude, Cristina's business quickly expanded to cater fashion events for designers like Eileen Fisher, weddings around the country, children's birthday parties, and more. Her delicious no bakems make an irresistible, show-stopping statement wherever they appear.

By day, Cristina is a publicist at a major publishing house, where she works with cookbook, lifestyle, and contemporary fiction titles. She simultaneously creates buzz for and gains inspiration from celebrity authors like Rachael Ray, Chloe Coscarelli, Carla Hall, Amy Hatvany, Sarah Pekkanen, and Jennifer Weiner.

Cristina lives in Williamsburg, Brooklyn, with her husband, Jeremy. Contrary to popular belief, their apartment does, in fact, have a working oven.

For more information visit nobakemakery.com.

Credit: Ozzy Garcia

Thank you for
stopping by
No Bake Makery!